LOVE IS
THE
ANSWER

W9-ARC-543

BOOKS BY GERALD JAMPOLSKY

Out of Darkness into the Light

To Give Is to Receive:
An 18 Day
Course on Healing Relationships

Love Is Letting Go of Fear

Teach Only Love

Goodbye to Guilt

One Person Can Make a Difference

AND ON BANTAM AUDIO CASSETTES:

To Give Is to Receive

Teach Only Love

Introduction to a Course in Miracles

Forgiveness Is the Key to Happiness

For information on Jerry Jampolsky's lecture and
workshop schedule as well as information on audio and video cassette tapes, please send a self
addressed envelope to:

Gerald G. Jampolsky, M.D.
c/o Mini Course
P.O. Box 1012
Tiburon, CA 94920

LOVE IS THE ANSWER

CREATING POSITIVE RELATIONSHIPS

Gerald G. Jampolsky, M.D.,
and
Diane V. Cirincione

A
BANTAM
TRADE
PAPERBACK

BANTAM BOOKS
NEW YORK · TORONTO · LONDON · SYDNEY · AUCKLAND

LOVE IS THE ANSWER
A Bantam Book
Bantam hardcover edition / May 1990
Bantam trade paperback edition / April 1991

All rights reserved.
Copyright © 1990 by Gerald G. Jampolsky, M.D. and
Diane V. Cirincione.
Cover art copyright © 1991 by Bantam Books.
Library of Congress Catalog Card Number: 89-18520.
No part of this book may be reproduced or transmitted
in any form or by any means, electronic or mechanical,
including photocopying, recording, or by any information
storage and retrieval system, without permission in
writing from the publisher.
For information address: Bantam Books.

ISBN 0-553-35268-7

Published simultaneously in the United States and Canada

Bantam Books are published by Bantam Books, a division of Bantam
Doubleday Dell Publishing Group, Inc. Its trademark, consisting of the
words "Bantam Books" and the portrayal of a rooster, is Registered in
U.S. Patent and Trademark Office and in other countries. Marca
Registrada. Bantam Books, 666 Fifth Avenue, New York, New York 10103.

PRINTED IN THE UNITED STATES OF AMERICA

RRH   0 9 8 7 6 5 4 3 2 1

We dedicate this book with boundless love and appreciation to our parents, Tillie and Leo Jampolsky, Thomas Cirincione, and Filomena Biele Girard and Lawrence Aime Girard. They have been our most significant teachers. We learned so many things in our relationships with them, including the power of love, acceptance, and forgiveness. We are grateful beyond words for each and every experience we have shared with them.

ACKNOWLEDGMENTS

With the deepest appreciation, we wish to thank the many people who have shared their lives with us. The way we have jointly learned from each of them is expressed in this book.

Our warm thanks and special gratitude go to our dear friend Hal Zina Bennett, who spent many helpful hours with us editing this book, and to Jack O. Keeler, for his wonderful illustrations portraying the concepts we present here.

Our special thanks and love go to Michelle Rapkin, our editor at Bantam, for her continued support and encouragement.

We wish to acknowledge that the foundation of this book is based on principles from *A Course in Miracles*, and we are most grateful to Judith Skutch Whitson and Robert Skutch of The Foundation for Inner Peace for their permission to quote from The Course. In some cases, we have used quotations from The Course as chapter titles. These are noted with asterisks in the table of contents.

Also, short quotations from The Course are centered on left-hand pages throughout the book. We include them because we have found them so helpful in understanding the principles we are presenting.

"A Course in Miracles" is published by The Foundation for Inner Peace, P. O. Box 635, Tiburon, California 94920.

CONTENTS

INTRODUCTION

This book is about healing relationships, all kinds of relationships. The principles we describe here apply to our relationships with our parents, children, spouses, lovers, relatives, friends, business associates, coworkers, and bosses. They are applicable in healing our relationships with ex-husbands and wives, teachers, students, the politicians whose decisions affect our lives, lawyers, physicians, and other professional people, as well as with anyone else whose lives we touch.

This book is also about healing our relationship with our planet Earth, with God, our Source, Nature, or whatever name you might give to that Force in the Universe that gives us all life. Equally important, this book is about healing our relationships with ourselves so that we can experience deep inner peace.

When we stop to look more closely at our lives and at the many serious challenges we face in our world today, it is not always easy to see that the number-one problem we face has to do with our relationships. We forget that relationship problems are not just isolated events, limited to difficulties we may be having in communicating with one another. Beyond this we are involved in "a relationship" with our whole environment, including plants, water, air, and all that nurtures and supports life on this planet.

Today, as a result of an increase in stress and fear in the world, we are seeing an alarming increase in drug abuse and addiction, physical and emotional abuse, incest, adolescent suicide, divorce, and one-parent families. There is increased concern and fear about acid rain, and the disappearing rain forests and ozone layer. Additionally, the AIDS crisis has created an epidemic of fear and hysteria that has increased feelings of separation and isolation.

Our relationships with each other, with our planet, and with the universe have never been more important. We have the wisdom to understand and control the impact of our actions on the Earth, yet we are doing so many things that threaten our environment and the health of future generations. We have the ability to join in peace and friendship in so many areas of our lives, yet the possibility for nuclear warfare still looms over all our heads. There are many who believe that the world is suffering from a critical illness, crying out for our help and our love, which can bring about its healing.

What is the illness that is causing so much suffering for our world, and what is the meaning of its cry for help? Mother Teresa has stated that the most significant ailment in the world today is "spiritual deprivation." It is a feeling of being unworthy of love, of feeling unlovable, of not having the capacity to give or to receive love, and of feeling that there is a wall separating us from ourselves, others, and that which created us.

Spiritual deprivation is a state of mind where we feel a sense of emptiness inside, and separated from the spiritual being that each of us truly is. It is a state of forgetfulness, of not remembering that who and what we are is love.

This book is based on the belief that we all have the capacity to retrain our minds to recognize that love is the most powerful healing force there is. As we recognize this, our interactions with the planet and its inhabitants will reflect that love.

This book is about hope, faith, trust, love, and forgiveness. It emphasizes that the good news is that the bad news is not true. It is about looking at all of our beliefs and asking ourselves if they are bringing us inner peace and happiness or if they are bringing us conflict, pain, and misery.

More and more people are beginning to feel that there must be another way of thinking, perceiving, and acting. And perhaps the beginning of another way of looking at the world is to reevaluate all of our beliefs. It is, after all, our beliefs that determine what we see, experience, and expect. When we are willing to take a new look at our own beliefs, we then have an opportunity to begin rediscovering who and what we are and to redetermine our true purpose on Earth.

When we have unhealed relationships in our lives, we take our feelings about them out on the world. If ever there was a time to ask our own hearts for help in finding another way of communicating with each other and for having loving relationships that last, it is now.

Although the world has made amazing advances in the fields of science, medicine, education, and electronic media, we still have a long way to go when it comes to having loving and harmonious communications in all of our relationships. We have made spectacular strides in exploring the moon and outer space; yet many of us are out of touch with, or have not substantially begun to explore, the inner spaces of the heart and mind.

In this book, we open doors for exploring the inner spaces of our minds, in order to bring light into the darkness of past hurts. We explore the mechanisms of the mind and the defenses we have created against love and peace. We look at ways of resolving unfinished business from the past. We find the value of letting go of guilt and fear, and the boundless benefits that come when we recognize that forgiveness is the key to happiness and that love is only experienced when we give it.

The Challenge Is That It Is Our Choice

This is a book about love and forgiveness. It is about learning to listen to the voice of love within our hearts, and it emphasizes that at any given moment, no matter what is happening in our lives, we can always choose love instead of fear.

In our personal lives it is not always easy to apply these concepts; but when we do apply them, they can have significant, often dramatic, positive effects on our relationships. Yet we still struggle, finding that each day presents us with new challenges and opportunities. The temptation to criticize ourselves and others is still there—we are not always successful in letting go of that temptation.

Every day gives us new opportunities which teach us that we alone are responsible for what we experience; that we can always choose to see ourselves not as victims but as people doing our best to love and let go, no longer judging others or condemning ourselves.

From deep in our hearts, we welcome you on this journey, hoping that through it we might all realize the boundless power of love that we each have within us, uniting us all as One, while recognizing together that no matter what the question, love is the answer.

ATTITUDINAL HEALING

To forgive is to heal.

ATTITUDINAL HEALING

Most of us experience tension in relationships that we know could be better. There is an inner part of our being that really *does* want to achieve peace with the people and problems getting us down. Fortunately, creating positive relationships begins with ourselves. What we believe, what we see, and what we experience depends directly on the thoughts we have in our minds.

We believe that *all* relationships can be healed, allowing us to feel the peace of mind we all seek. This can be achieved through a "psychological-spiritual" approach based on the principles of Attitudinal Healing. Attitudinal Healing is the process of letting go of the fearful, guilty, angry, negative thoughts that so many of us carry in our minds. It is based on the premise that it is not other people or circumstances that cause us to be upset, but rather our own thoughts and attitudes *about* those people and circumstances that cause us distress.

In Attitudinal Healing, health is defined as "inner peace" and healing as "letting go of fear." It is a way of correcting our own misperceptions. Perhaps the most valuable gift

3

given to us by the universe is the freedom to choose and to decide upon our thoughts.

By using the principles of Attitudinal Healing presented in this book, we can learn to use free will to choose our thoughts. By exercising our ability to choose, we can let go of all illusions that create separation, such as the illusion that we can achieve happiness by getting other people to change in order to fit our own molds, so that we might feel "in control and safe." We can let go of fearful, negative, and guilty thoughts that limit our relationships and cause us to feel separate.

In this book, we will talk about two ways of looking at the world. One is through the eyes of the ego, and the other is through the eyes of love. We can always choose whether we are going to listen to the voice of the ego or to the voice of love. We create positive relationships only when we listen to the voice of love.

Each of us was born with the power and capacity to

There is another way of looking at the world

accept love, to love unconditionally, and to bring love into all of our relationships. It is our investment in the ego that blocks our awareness of love's presence. In this book we will describe how it is possible to let go of our attachment to the voice of the ego and start listening to the voice of love.

The Ego and Its Defenses Against Love

You will find that when we talk about the ego, our concept of it is a little different from that of most psychologists and psychiatrists. We define the ego as the part of us that believes that our identity is limited to a body and personality-self, born only to die. It denies that we have a spiritual identity, a self that is not limited by physical form. The ego often speaks to us as that chattering internal voice that criticizes and judges other people and ourselves. It is the source of much negativity in our lives.

The ego's main message is fear—fear that we are all alone, abandoned in a world of scarcity and that we must seek but never find what we are looking for. The ego sees the world as a place of separation, of separate bodies and separate minds and separate hearts. It does not believe in wholeness or oneness. It does not know the meaning of love, and sees peace as its enemy. It encourages us to believe that love can only be built by thinking of our own selfish needs first.

As a substitute for love and as a way of keeping love away from us, the ego entices us to make idols and gods of all sorts of things, from bodies, sex, drugs, suffering, gambling, failure, guilt, and money to an endless list of objects in our outer world. It does not want us to explore our inner world and heart to find our spiritual being. It wants us to be afraid of God and to believe that either there is no

God or, if there is one, it must be a God that rewards us for good behavior and, at any moment, can be cruel and punish us.

The ego tells us to be demanding and willing to walk all over other people to get what we want. It tells us to keep remembering that anger and fear are justified, that these ways of behaving get us what we want and that "attack" and "defense" are the best ways of protecting ourselves and our families.

To gain still more understanding of how the ego blocks us from the awareness of love's presence, let us imagine that we are listening to the voice of the ego at its "central control." What we hear might go something like this:

The purpose of relationships is to meet my personal needs, to have my own interests come before the welfare of others, even if it causes feelings of separation. I want instant gratification in my relationships, and physical and sexual gratification are at the top of my list.

I never want any criticism or disagreement from anyone. I want my way at all times, and I want to be liked, loved, and accepted even when my behavior is hostile, obnoxious, or attacking.

The purpose of all relationships is to show you and everyone else that I'm the one with the power. What I say goes. Remember, if there ever is a lack of harmony in our relationship, I am always right and you are always wrong. And I really want you to realize that if there is ever any problem in our relationship, you are the cause of it and the one to blame.

The ego goes on to say:

There is a double standard that makes it okay for me to be possessive, jealous, controlling, and manipulative. At the same time, it's okay for me to be dishonest, deceptive, to keep secrets from you, and to have affairs. But none of these things are okay for you to do.

I make the laws in all relationships, and one of my primary laws is that it is unforgivable for you to do anything that I don't want you to do.

The ego looks at relationships in a very negative way. It sees them as dangerous and as potential enemies. It would have us concentrate on differences, rather than similarities, and tell us to look upon differences as potential sources of deep hurt in our lives.

The ego tells us to never let go of past hurts because it is absolutely crucial to forever remember just how dangerous relationships can be. It would have us believe that without fear, we would not know how to protect ourselves and, therefore, would not know how to be safe and secure.

The Belief System of Love

Love looks at the world very differently. From the standpoint of the spiritual self, which is pure love, the purpose of our relationships is to experience a joining with one another and to remember that love is the only true reality there is. Within the belief system of love, we see that the purpose of our relationships is to remember who we are and that the essence of each of us is love. Rather than focusing on individual differences, love focuses on the similarities and the things that we, as spiritual beings, each have in common.

Love sees relationships as opportunities for learning and

as challenges for our personal growth. Rather than having us see relationships as fearful and dangerous, it helps us see them as possibilities for love and learning and that through them we might see the face of God in the other person, reminding us of our own holiness.

Love is changeless. It asks no questions and makes no judgments. It is always gentle and tender. It is always unfolding, extending, and expanding beyond all limitations. As we choose the belief system of love, rather than the belief system of the ego, we once again discover that happiness is our natural inheritance and our natural state of being.

The Bridge

How do we transform ourselves? How do we let go of the ego's belief system and begin to accept the belief system of love? The answer is simple, but our egos may try to tell us that it is too difficult.

The answer can be found in the "Bridge of Forgiveness." The foundation for this bridge is built on the very soil of love, where no one can do anything that is unforgivable. As we cross this bridge we discover that everyone is deserving of our total love, and we can learn to let go of the blocks of our ego perceptions so that we can once again love each other, ourselves, and the source of all life unconditionally.

To walk across the Bridge of Forgiveness is to walk the most important Bridge in the Universe, the bridge that can lead us to love, peace, and happiness beyond our wildest dreams. Though our egos will do their very best to distract us from seeing it, the Bridge of Forgiveness is always there, inviting us to cross it, guaranteeing us that in so doing, our relationships will become healed and we will experience more love and peace than we have ever before imagined.

The journey across this bridge, which we describe in the pages that follow, is filled with boundless joy and hope, as we rediscover the love and forgiveness that always abides in the heart and that heals all our relationships.

Forgiveness is the key to happiness

WHAT ARE RELATIONSHIPS FOR?

Use no relations to hold you to the past,
but with each one each day be born again.
A minute, even less, will be enough
to free you from the past.

WHAT ARE RELATIONSHIPS FOR?

As we have traveled and talked with people the world over, we have found many men and women who are successful in the ways of the world, with many accomplishments in their lives. Some have even achieved great fame and fortune. And yet, even with all their achievements, they are saying to themselves, "There's got to be more to life than this!" Regardless of how many things they have managed to get for themselves and their families, they are still left with feelings of emptiness.

Many are beginning to question whether they have had the right goals in life. Often they have been running fast, dealing with a lot of stress, and they have found very little time for living in the present. Often much of their focus has been money, not love. Many have become workaholics—working hard, performing very well in the world so that they can be the kind of good performer that they believe would please their parents. They are so busy performing that they have had little time for experiencing intimacy.

Many of us have large numbers of friends; but we find that there are few, if any, people in our lives with whom we feel we can share everything in our hearts. Some of us have been working very hard at careers, but in our personal lives, love and deep intimacy have always remained just a little beyond reach.

Perhaps we have had the wrong goals and have not been clear about our life's purpose. Maybe one of the main reasons that relationships have not been satisfying for many of us is that we have not been clear in our own minds about the *purpose* of our relationships. It seems to be an issue that we simply do not address very often. And when we do attempt to address it, our answers turn out to be rather vague.

To understand relationships, to have some better sense of how to make them work, it is essential to have a clear understanding about what relationships are for.

In the thought system of love, the goal of life is inner peace, and the true purpose of all of our relationships is to join. If we believe in our hearts that when two or more people come together the real purpose is joining, then certain dynamics are set into motion that can bring peace, harmony, and love into that relationship.

In the thought system of the world, that is, the thought system of the ego, the purpose of relationships is separation. Separation has its own set of dynamics, which puts conflict, disharmony, fear, and mistrust into motion.

In this book we will be contrasting these two belief systems—the belief system of love and the belief system of the ego—so that we can make clearer choices about which thought system we want to believe.

Seeing Our Own Lives More Clearly

Sometimes the best way to learn about ourselves is to imagine having to explain what our lives are about to a person who knows nothing about us. For example, let us imagine what it would be like if people from another planet came to visit us on Earth and asked us what relationships are for.

What might they see, and what questions might they ask us as they started looking around our planet? For example, the visitors might walk into a department store and see a customer talking to a clerk, blaming that clerk for selling a piece of merchandise that was faulty. What might the visitors from outer space think this was all about? They might say to themselves, "Well, I guess one of the things that relationships are for is to find someone to yell at when you don't get exactly what you want."

The same visitors walk into the workplace and see Joe, a manager, chewing out Barbara, an employee whose production is low for that month. Instead of talking with her about ways that she might improve, Joe threatens to fire Barbara if she doesn't increase her production in two weeks. From this, the visitors might say to themselves, "I guess relationships are also for finding someone to blame and make guilty when you don't meet your production quota."

Next, the visitors go into a typical home and see Richard, the father of twelve-year-old Michael, getting angry at his son who just came home with a *D* on his report card. From this the visitors decide that "in relationships you must grasp every opportunity to measure and judge other people. Then you give them your love when they perform in the way you want them to and you withdraw your love when they don't perform so well."

One real puzzle to our visitors from outer space would surely be how we value and use *justified anger*, guilt, and blame in our relationships. They would surely find people who believed that some things that happen in life are unforgivable. They might, for example, find Juanita, a woman who has not spoken to her sister for twenty years "because she embarrassed me in front of my boyfriend when we were teenagers." From this, the visitors might decide that "relationships can be used to cling to very old, painful experiences and to punish those who we feel are responsible."

Or let's say that the visitors look at a present relationship where one person blames another for things that happened in past relationships. Perhaps a person had a difficult childhood, a parent who took away privileges every time he did something the parent didn't like. Having grown to adulthood, the person who suffered this kind of treatment with a parent now punishes his own wife and children in the same way. From this, our visitors from outer space might decide that relationships are for treating other people in the same terrible ways you were treated as a child.

Suppose that these visitors from another planet had the ability to see inside our minds. Let's say that they could literally read our thoughts. So they use their ability to look into our minds and discover that we are always judging ourselves. We are always thinking that we are not talented enough or beautiful enough or rich enough or even loving enough.

Looking a little further, they might see that we use our self-judgments in our relationships. The visitors might notice that we frequently, often unwittingly, look for other people who have those same traits that we dislike in ourselves, and we then criticize them and put them down. From this, the visitors might decide that relationships are for finding someone who is most like what we perceive as the worst part of ourselves and then we attack them for being like us.

The visitors might also decide that in our relationships on Earth we use other people as screens for projecting onto others the feelings that we do not want to look at in ourselves. For example, the visitors meet a very talented man named Dennis, who has just created a wonderful computer software program that will help everyone in business. As a child, Dennis had a father who was always criticizing him and telling him that his ideas were no good. Even though Dennis has created this wonderful new software program and knows how well it works, he still holds on to the notion that his ideas are no good. Just as he is about to put the program on the market, he shows it to a college professor he knows, who tells him it is no good. Dennis gets very depressed and for a long time he convinces himself that the old professor is right.

The visitors from outer space see something that Dennis doesn't see. They see that he is attached to failure and feeling inadequate, and he has accepted a limitation that his father placed on him many years ago: that his ideas are no good, no matter who says anything to the contrary. They also see that Dennis actually went out and found a relationship, with the college professor, where he could continue to act like a fearful, inadequate child. The professor's role was to enable Dennis to hold on to that self-limitation.

After looking at a great many relationships, the visitors from outer space might get together, talk things over and finally decide that the purpose of relationships here on Earth is to create separation between people. People use relationships to maintain fear, guilt and a sense of heaviness and loneliness in their lives.

Relationships Are for Joining

When we make the decision that every relationship that we have is for joining, whether it is a casual meeting with a new person, someone we have known for years, or a relative who has been in our life since birth, we begin to experience a growing and expanding inner peace. When we see everyone we meet as a new teacher, helping us to learn what forgiveness is all about, we can begin to understand and experience the meaning of infinite patience.

We can retrain our minds to perceive every person we may meet, in any situation and regardless of the circumstances, as a new opportunity for our own personal growth. We can learn to let go of our investment in our ego and its judgments and recognize that all relationships offer us the opportunity to join with others and to experience and love one another as well as ourselves.

PART 3

SEVEN STEPPING STONES FOR CREATING MORE POSITIVE RELATIONSHIPS

Love will enter immediately
into any mind that truly wants it,
but it must want it truly.

INTRODUCTION

In this part of the book we present "Seven Stepping Stones" that describe a pathway to loving relationships. Before going on, we thought it might be helpful to explain how these can help you create more loving relationships in your life.

The Stepping Stones help us to find the way past what we call "blocks" to love. Blocks are the ego's defenses against love, and our egos will do everything in their power to get us off the pathway to love and to block our awareness of love. The blocks of the ego include guilt, fear, blame, mistrust, unforgiveness, feelings of being unworthy of love, trying to control other people, being stuck in the past, jealousy, possessiveness, and competition—to name just a few that we'll discuss here. Our egos manufacture blocks to hide our own anger and hurt feelings from our awareness, making it difficult for us to see that the real problems, and their solutions, are within us.

Blocks put us in a state of limited awareness, causing us to forget that the love we seek from others already lies in abundance within ourselves. They cause us to feel separate and alone, creating illusions that when we are feeling a lack of love it is because we are living in a world where there is a scarcity of love. They frequently create a heavy fog around us, making us feel lost, confused, and abandoned.

Each of the Seven Stepping Stones presented here is designed to help clear away the blocks. When we become absolutely and totally committed to peace and love, these blocks begin to vanish. We then see love, and that is all that we see.

In our own lives, as well as in our workshops and lectures, we have found that it is almost as if the Seven Stepping Stones are illuminated by bright beacons, guiding us along a path where we come out of the darkness and fog created by our blocks into the brilliant light created by the presence of love.

As you read this part of the book, finding new clarity about the blocks in your own life, and finding the Stepping Stones for moving quickly beyond them, it would be helpful to imagine yourself moving along a clear path that spirals up a hill into a beautiful lush garden filled with light, peace, and tranquillity. This image represents our true state of mind.

Move from one Stepping Stone to another at whatever pace you find comfortable, giving yourself plenty of time to allow the principles described to become part of your awareness. It may be helpful to pause at each Stepping Stone to think of ways that the concepts you have just read might be applied for dissolving blocks in any of your relationships right now. With every heartbeat and breath, allow yourself to commit to making these Stepping Stones part of your being.

In the garden you are moving toward, you will find peace and a oneness with nature, where there is total harmony and inter-connectedness. As you move from one Stepping Stone to the next, each one revealing a fuller picture of the garden, remind yourself to walk slowly, since love is never in a hurry.

The Stepping Stones on this path lead to a new commitment to really listen to others with patience and without judgment, as we find ourselves leaving behind any value we once found in holding on to one of our blocks. A good example would be our past grievances, which create the false illusion that there is value in fighting and attacking one another.

The Stepping Stones lead us to a new awareness of how we can heal our relationships with ourselves, our parents, our spouses and lovers, our children, and everyone we have ever known, whether they are living or not. Here we can find a new understanding of forgiveness, which allows us to let go of any blame for past hurts without condoning or feeling we must tolerate another person's negative behavior.

These Stepping Stones can help us to look past the physical body and the disguises our egos tell us to wear, so that we may choose to see only the light of innocence and love in everyone we meet. They mark a path where we have a new opportunity to change our ways of looking at the world. With each new step we take on this path, it becomes increasingly clear that no matter what the problem, no matter how hopeless we may feel, love is the answer. With each step we take we become more fully alive as we embrace the world with tenderness, gentleness, compassion, and limitless love.

1

MOVING PAST OUR ILLUSIONS AND PERCEPTIONS

Illusions of Love

In order to learn how to create positive loving relationships in our lives, it is important to understand that what often seems like love may actually be an illusion of love. Illusions of love are created by the ego, which is interested only in getting its own selfish needs met.

Illusions of love take many different forms. For example, when both people's selfish needs are met in a relationship, the ego feels as if it is on top of the world. Most of us have experienced this as the "honeymoon period" of a relationship, an illusion that is the basis for "romantic love." This illusion lasts only as long as both people's needs are being met, and when either feels that his or her needs are not met, one or both parties become frustrated, and this frustration can quickly turn into anger.

What had looked like love just a while ago has now become a love/hate relationship. Whether we use words or not, we send to each other a message that "I will love you only so long as you give me what I want." This is the basis of the illusion we call "conditional love."

The ego knows fear, but it neither understands nor is able to experience love. The ego's form of love is always conditional and is always an illusion. It's favorite theme is "I will love you if . . ." The emphasis, of course, is on the "if."

Through our egos we may put out thousands of these "ifs," or conditions on our love. As parents, we may send the message to our children that "I will love you if you get good grades at school, but I will withdraw my love if you bring home bad grades."

There are some parents who, under the guise of love, say to their child as they start to beat him, "This is going to hurt me more than it hurts you. I am only hitting you for your own good, only because I love you." In this way, parents teach fear rather than love and compassion. Much of the violence we see in adults comes from those who suffered physical abuse when they were children.

Conditional love in families may be seen when a wife sends a message to her husband that "I will love you only if you start spending more time with the family." Or perhaps the husband says, "I will love you if you have sex with me tonight, and I will reject you if you don't."

The ego is ambivalent about love and doesn't see sex as a way of sharing feelings of love, tenderness, caring, and gentleness toward another person. Rather, it sees sex as a trade or bargain and an opportunity for controlling and manipulating another person to serve its own selfish needs. It may use sex as a form of anger by communicating "I am angry at you, so I'll punish you by not having sex with you."

It may also use sex as a token to trade for financial security, the silent message being "I don't love you, but having sex with you is a way of holding on to you and the security that your money offers me." The ego is very good at creating these illusions of love, and it is capable of putting sex and love in separate compartments, completely dissociated from one another.

Sexual relationships can give the illusion of love when they may have nothing to do with love. They may be focused not on giving love to another person but only on getting one's own bodily needs satisfied. This is why in many relationships sex becomes boring. When we dissociate sex from love, sexual relations often become so mechanical that it is like two robots trying to communicate with each other, completely devoid of feelings.

The ego is quick to use categories of sexual behavior as a way of judging other people and withholding love. For example, instead of seeing that we don't have to agree with a person's life-style to accept them as they are, the ego may try to tell us that we should attack anyone whose sexual preference may differ from ours. Often the ego uses this form of categorizing and judging as a way of projecting its own fears, homophobia (fear of homosexuality), for example, outside itself. It does this by labeling a homosexual person as an enemy, judging him or her as not worthy of receiving anything but hostility.

When it comes to love, the ego believes that we always suffer from great scarcity. Relationships simply don't work when they are based on this illusion. The ego's image is that we have a "gas tank" for love, and its gauge is always hovering around empty, causing us to be constantly looking for a refill.

Although the ego does not want us to love ourselves, it would have us seek others to love us. It is much more interested in getting love than giving it. It frequently guides us into relationships where we have the illusion of getting something from the other person that is missing in ourselves. These are illusions of love based on a bargain or trade, such as "I will be the strong one and make all the decisions if you promise never to criticize me or reject me."

The ego has an almost unlimited capacity for creating illusions of love, but all of them are based on controlling and manipulating other people in order to get its own needs met. The ego has absolutely no interest in, nor capacity for, unconditional love, where there is total acceptance, where there are no assumptions, expectations, or demands, and where there is no desire to "get something" from the other person.

Unconditional love does not mean supporting another person's insanity or condoning hurtful behavior. It means a willingness to see past the body and its behavior and to choose to see the essence of love that is the spiritual being of that person. Unconditional love, however, does not mean that you simply put up with another person's behavior no matter what.

This concept is frequently misunderstood. For example, a woman may be married to an alcoholic who physically and emotionally abuses her, and yet she stays in that situation, where she continues to get punished. The wife may think she is staying because of love, but that is an illusion of love. Often that person stays in an abusive situation out of fear and a deep-seated guilt, where she unconsciously believes that she somehow deserves the beatings she receives.

A person with healthy self-esteem who also loves unconditionally does not stay in an abusive situation. The true essence of love is experienced not with illusions of love

Conditional love   **Unconditional love**

based on the drive to "get," nor on illusions of love based on punishment of any kind. Unconditional love refers to the "content" of our love rather than the "form." It means accepting the love of our spiritual self and choosing to look beyond the body and personality-self of the other person to see the spiritual essence within him or her.

Projection: As We Think, So We See

As the cartoon character Pogo once said, "We have met the enemy and the enemy is us." The conflicts that we face in life are within our minds. They appear to be outside us only because our egos project our inner thoughts outward. It then appears that the enemy is outside us.

Every time we allow ourselves to be convinced that the cause of everything that happens is outside us, we fuel the ego. To hide the fact that our thoughts create our reality, our egos make use of their favorite mechanism, *projection*, which tricks us into believing that: (1) everything going on in our lives is happening outside us; (2) every person in the world has a separate mind and there is no way that we can ever experience our minds joined as one; and (3) we are victims rather than creators of our relationships.

The ego's projections are not easy for us to recognize. When someone is angry at us, we usually choose to experience them as attacking us. From the ego's point of view, that person is a reality outside us and has nothing at all to do with the hidden thoughts in our own minds. We create an illusion of separation by "proving" that the other person is wrong and we are right. In truth, our feelings of being attacked are inside us, actually coming from our own inner battles with our own conflicted thoughts.

This is how it works: Imagine, if you will, that your mind

is like a projector in a movie theater. It works the same way for all of us. It is as though all our past hurts, loves, joys, disappointments, attacks, etc., are recorded on film, stored in the archives of our memory banks. Something that happens to us in the present can call forth these old films and pretty soon we are projecting them onto the present.

For example, an authority figure may get angry at us. We may feel hurt and rejected, and these feelings may call up old hidden memories of similar conflicts that we may have had with our parents, or a teacher, or perhaps a former employer. Pretty soon we are projecting these old films onto the present. The present and the past become fused as one. This prevents us from seeing the present as it truly is.

The people in the present are different than the people in our films from the past, but the themes are the same. Our minds project the old films onto people in the present, filtered through our lenses of unresolved conflicts from the past. When we project to the outside world in this way, we end up seeing a world that actually originated in our own minds.

As long as we listen only to the ego, we will not see other people for who and what they really are. Rather, the ego will see every person and every experience in our lives as a giant, blank movie screen, upon which it will project our feelings and thoughts from the past. The ego tries to make the present invisible to us.

How is it that two people, experiencing the same angry person, can have two such completely different responses to that person? One finds little or no difficulty making the relationship work, going on to resolve the problem between them. The other feels frustrated and angry, convinced that the relationship is impossible. One person may see an attacking, angry person, someone who is trying to hurt them. The other may see the same person not as attacking at all but as fearful and giving a call of help for love.

The result of projection is always the same: "As we think, so we see." Angry, unloving thoughts project an angry, unloving world, filled with angry, unloving relationships. Loving and peaceful thoughts extend out from our hearts and minds, creating a world of loving and peaceful relationships.

When we begin to see that we truly do project our thoughts, feelings and old conflicts out onto the world, and when we begin to understand that we can choose what we think, then we are in a position to finally see that we are not victims of our relationships at all. We are only victims of our own thoughts, and we really do have a choice in the matter.

We can retrain our minds to have only loving and peaceful thoughts, a choice we can make anew every moment of every day. When we do this, we are taking responsibility for our own projections and our relationships, choosing to create positive and loving ones and succeeding in that.

Perception Is a Mirror, Not a Fact

Most of us go through life following the ego's guidance, which wants us to believe that our perceptions of the world are accurate pictures of how the world outside us really is. Our egos want us to believe that what we perceive is the direct result of what our eyes and ears and other senses tell us.

Much of the time, we mistakenly believe that our thoughts and feelings are caused by events in the world around us. We tend to believe that if something is going wrong in our lives, the cause is "out there."

If we choose to believe only in our own perceptions, it will appear to us that our reality is made up only of form, time, and space. This means that it will seem to us that our lives consist only of our physical bodies, taking up a certain amount of space, existing in a particular location, lasting only a certain number of years, and oriented according to past, present, and future.

As long as we hold on to this way of looking at the world, our perceptions of reality will be constantly changing, always turned this way and that by events outside us. The foundation of the ego's belief system is that we are each separate and alone in a world where there is no such thing as unity where hearts and minds are joined.

We don't want to believe that what we see and what we hear are projections of what we think. We deny that what we think is what we see, and that it is our beliefs that determine what we think.

The ego does everything it can to prevent us from understanding that our thoughts, not the outside world, *cause* what we see and experience, and that the world we experience is the *effect* of our own thoughts. When we let the ego trick us into believing otherwise, our thinking about the world and how our perceptions work is actually upside down.

Looking at these things we might find ourselves wondering: "What does perception have to do with my relationships? What does it have to do with conflicts? How can it be that other people just don't see the world as I do?"

Since no two people have exactly the same thoughts and experiences, they cannot possibly perceive in the same way. This causes many communication difficulties in relationships.

As long as we think that what we see with our eyes and hear with our ears is true, we will believe that everyone is exactly the same. But relationships go awry when we expect others to perceive, assimilate, and react exactly as we do. When something happens that proves we're not the same, our egos tell us to argue, cajole, and in every way possible try to convince the other person that their view of the world

Perception is a mirror, not a fact

is wrong and ours is right. When we fail to get agreement that we are right, we frequently become disillusioned and upset, with deep feelings of separation. We may even believe that love is only possible if two people's perceptions match perfectly.

In summary, perception is what we experience as a result of projecting thoughts and feelings from the mind outward. What we think we see with our eyes is actually a mirror of our internal thoughts.

Healing the Split Mind

The Split Mind

The split mind is one that attempts to obey the laws of the ego and respond to the laws of love at the same time. But no matter how hard we try, this can't be done. When we allow our minds to be split, we end up creating conflicts, chaos, inconsistency, and disharmony in our relationships.

For example, in the course of a busy day, it would not be unusual for some of us to be carrying on a perfectly pleasant conversation with someone at the same time we are thinking: "Oh, I simply can't stand this person. He reminds me of a teacher I had in high school, whom I never did like." We are disguising ourselves, pretending to like this person, while all along we have these secret thoughts that keep the two of us very separate.

When our minds are split, we not only deceive the other person; we deceive ourselves. The result is a battle within ourselves. Our opposing thoughts and behaviors create chaos and confusion. The self-deception of the split mind causes us to feel guilty, and we end up being anything but loving toward the other person and toward ourselves.

The ego uses "compartmentalization" to keep us unaware of

the deceptions of our own split minds. It is as if the ego builds steel walls within the mind, sealing off separate vaults, filling them with our opposing thoughts and feelings, so that there can be no communication between one part of the mind and another. The ego itself is sealed away in just such a compartment so that it never knows the part of the mind that is filled only with love.

A truly loving relationship is an enemy of the ego, which will do anything to bring about conflict and run away from peace. The deceptive ego will project onto other people our own mistrust of ourselves, convincing us that it is very difficult to truly trust another person completely.

Our belief in fear and guilt keeps the mind split. Our belief that we have done something that deserves to be punished keeps our ego's thought system alive. As long as we hold on to these beliefs, our egos blanket us with curtains of darkness, hiding the inner light of love that is our true reality.

One of the ego's laws is that we should base all our decisions on negative experiences from the past, and that we can accurately predict the present and future in this way. The ego's laws say that love is always conditional and that we should never trust anything we can't see, taste, smell, touch, hear, or measure. To follow the laws of the ego, we must always maintain the belief that we are all separate, our lives limited to our bodies, and that sooner or later we will experience frustration, pain, unhappiness, despair, fear, hopelessness, and finally death.

When our minds are split, our egos are focused on "getting" and having multiple goals and wishes that frequently conflict not only with other people's goals but with our own. Confusion and despair are the result of following the laws of the ego and the split mind.

**The split mind has little room
for love**

**The mind that is whole
is full of love, leaving no
room for the ego**

Healing the Split Mind

Love has a different set of laws, and these laws teach us that love is always unconditional, changeless, maximal, and all-inclusive. Unconditional love has no limits and no boundaries. When we follow the inner teacher of love, we live as if the present moment is the only moment there is, and that it is a timeless moment in which no guilt or fear can be found.

When we allow our lives to be guided by love, we make all our decisions by listening to our inner teacher, which is the voice of love. When we think only loving thoughts, the confusion and conflict of the split mind ceases to be, and we once again feel connected with our Source.

When love is pure and consistent, we judge neither ourselves nor others. We feel no need to interpret the motives or behavior of others. We have no need to be fault finders or to put other people into categories to make them separate and different, alienated from the rest of us.

When our minds are healed and whole, we are tranquil and open, filled only with loving thoughts, and we find harmony and peace in everything we do.

We feel no conflict or inner battle with what we ourselves are thinking, feeling, saying, and doing. All our thoughts and feelings are congruent. Our relationships become loving and harmonious, and this love expands, extending out into the world.

To heal the split mind, there are three positive statements that we can say to ourselves that can be immediately helpful:

1. "I recognize that my mind is split."

Whenever we are not feeling totally peaceful, happy, and loving, we are experiencing symptoms of the split mind. We may be feeling anxiety, irritability, anger, doubt, worry, resentment, or depression, just to name a few.

2. "I am willing to change my thoughts."

We begin to change when we stop finding value in the thoughts and emotions causing us conflict. Since we are the only ones who ever put thoughts in our own minds, we can always change those thoughts. We can choose happiness and inner peace. The mind becomes whole again when we are willing to live one second at a time, having only loving and peaceful thoughts.

3. "I am willing to forgive."

Whenever we become aware of having the symptoms of a split mind, we can be certain that we are condemning or judging others or ourselves. By letting go of our judgmental and condemning thoughts, we automatically find forgiveness. It is our forgiveness that dissolves the compartments that the ego has created in the mind, and as soon as the compartments are gone our misperceptions disappear. We then become aware that love is our only reality, and our minds are whole again, filled with the love that we carry out into all our relationships.

The root of all our relationship problems is the unforgiving mind, which causes us to feel separated from our true identity, which is love. We can choose forgiveness, dissolving the compartments of the split mind, and in doing so we can heal our relationships.

I Am Never Upset
for the Reasons I Think

Most of us are familiar with the scenario of the father who comes home from work and explodes the moment he puts

Honesty is when there is harmony in what you think, say, and do

his foot in the door. He rages at his wife because dinner is going to be late. He is furious with his children for making such a mess of the house. He feels very self-righteous in his anger, considering it completely justified.

This man has no conscious awareness that his upset has nothing to do with the late dinner or the messy house. His upset comes from events that occurred long before he got home.

Like many of us, this father has put a steel wall around his memories of what happened earlier that day. The fact is that his boss called him on the carpet that day for being late to work too often and warned him that if he continued being late he would lose his job.

This man also had a painful, repressed memory from his childhood that was stirred up by his confrontation with his boss. When he was a child, his own father was always on his back for being late for dinner and tardy for school, and he still felt guilt over that. As so many of us do, this man denied his own guilt and then looked for other people in his life to blame.

Whenever he perceived a problem, his ego convinced him that he was not "the guilty one." Instead, it convinced him that the guilty one was whichever person he believed was deserving of his blame at that moment.

As long as we project onto other people, we will feel that we don't have to deal with the intolerable pain of our own guilt. So we continue to deny our own guilt and project it outward. These projections are actually the images of "old films" of events that occurred in the past.

Let us explore this further. The ego, which we can control, always believes that we are separate and alone in the world and that the cause of our distress is always what comes to us through our eyes and other senses. To the ego, blame for our upset always comes from outside us. But the fact is that what happens is quite the opposite.

Our egos take everything that comes from our senses and filters it through our vast memory bank of past experiences, condemning judgments, and guilt. This is all hidden from our conscious awareness. We then project what comes through the ego's filter out onto other people. These projections become our perceptions, creating the illusion that the causes for our upsets are always outside us.

Out of these projections we create battles with other people, ignoring the fact that the real battle is with the conflicting thoughts in our own minds. The ego, that great distorter and master of denial, makes it extremely difficult for us to see all this, hiding from us the reality that we are never upset for the reasons we think.

The ego's way of filtering and interpreting everything that comes through our senses causes us to feel separate from each other, and makes it most difficult to have loving relationships.

When you feel upset, it can be helpful to just stop for a moment and remind yourself that we are never upset for the reasons we think. With this in mind, it becomes possible to stop our projections and begin uncovering our unfinished business from the past. We can do this by asking the following question: "When, where, and with whom have I experienced this same feeling before?"

Often, as we delve further, we discover that we have been in similar circumstances and have experienced similar feelings many times before. By going further and further back, we come to the real source of our conflict, which is an unhealed relationship that we are still holding on to from very early in our lives. We discover, also, that as we look at these relationships and heal them, we will be free of them, no longer projecting them onto the present.

When we are in conflict in our present relationships, real healing can come only by reminding ourselves that our upset is based on projections from past experiences. They could have happened a few minutes ago or even many years ago. The healing of our present conflicts comes from healing our past and remembering that we are never upset for the reasons we think.

2

_____

TRANSFORMING FEAR, BLAME, AND GUILT INTO LOVE

The Universal Fear

On the deepest of levels, our biggest fear—and the root of all problems in our relationships—is our fear of death. We may experience this universal fear as our fear of love and intimacy, as a fear of separation from a person we love, or even as a fear of God, or the presence of a Higher Power.

The root of this universal fear is the ego's belief system, which equates the body with life. The ego believes that our only reality *is* the ego and our physical being. It denies the reality of our spiritual essence, which equates love with life and knows that love is eternal. We continue to experience this universal fear only as long as we adhere to the ego's belief that when the body dies that is the end of life.

Our egos give us many confusing messages about this universal fear. They tell us: "Seek love but be afraid of it, because you will gradually be separated from love by death or rejection." When we give our ego our full allegiance by buying into the belief that death is to be greatly feared, we also become afraid of love and of being separated from those we hold dear. So many of our relationship problems are based on this fear of separation, and on the belief that sooner or later the one we love will die or leave us and we will be all alone.

Many of the control issues that make our relationships so

difficult have to do with our ego's fear of death and feelings of helplessness about how to deal with this fear. The ego tries to convince us that there is only one way to deal with this fear, and that is to somehow control death. Since this is an impossible goal, the ego ends up feeling helpless. This feeling becomes part of our false perception. Trying to control other people is one of the more obvious ways the ego has of warding off its own fear of not having any control over death.

Within this context, we experience a deep fear of love, and we block love by trying to control each other. Even though it may be possible to manipulate other people for a while, it is never possible to completely control them. However, the ego would have us believe that it is indeed possible to do so, and it encourages us to spend our energies on this instead of on love.

The ego's ultimate expression of its fear of its own death is often found in our fear of God. We experience this in many different ways, among them being our fear and anger at the world and at God, as well as our denial of the existence of God.

We have known parents whose fear of their own deaths, as well as the deaths of their children, was so great that they separated themselves emotionally from their loved ones as a way of protecting themselves from the pain they believed they would one day have to endure.

The fear of death and our perception of being separated from love or a Higher Power can take many different forms. For example, many of us avoid talking about death and making out a will because it is such a painful subject. We perpetuate this fear and avoidance as long as we adhere to the ego's belief that when the body dies that is the end of life.

For many of us it doesn't seem possible that the fear of losing someone you love could be the same fear as getting hit by a car or the fear of your business failing. They appear different from one another.

Looking more closely, however, the greatest fear underlying the possible loss of a loved one is the fear of *separation* from him or her. For instance, the parents whose child has a life-threatening illness are most afraid of being separated from that child through death; the person whose partner or spouse falls in love with another person fears the pain of separation from that relationship. Likewise, people addicted to alcohol or other drugs may be afraid of being rejected and therefore separated from their families and society.

Underlying all fears of separation lies our fear of feeling separate from ourselves and the Loving Force that created us all. The possibility of being hit by a car creates the immediate fear of being *separate* from our current state of health and our life. Losing a business looks quite different;

The wall that my mind has built keeps me separate

yet businesses are often perceived as extensions of ourselves, and the threat of their loss is the fear of *separation*
from our own creativity as well as part of our personal
identity.

The fear of separation underlies each and every problem
in our lives and creates many deep fears of intimacy and
closeness. How we look at separation, death, and life, and
whether separation is a truth or an illusion, is determined
by our belief systems.

Are we just bodies and personalities that walk for a brief
time on this planet Earth, where life ends in death, and
where our egos perceive an infinity of separations? Or are
we the essence of love, spiritual beings who are always
joined with each other and a Higher Power, where there is
no separation and where the spiritual essence of our being
is eternal?

When we choose to look beyond the body and no longer
believe in death or perceive it as the end of life, it can do
much to enhance and create positive loving relationships,
relationships that have an absence of fear. People in these
relationships are not fearful of separation because their belief systems allow them to feel joined and connected with
the Source of love at all times. They do not believe in the
ego's reality of separation.

Each day we have an opportunity to look at our belief
systems and to choose once again what we believe and what
will bring us peace and happiness.

Negative Thoughts

A disciplined mind is a free mind because it has the ability
to choose its contents and directions. Most of us have very
undisciplined minds, containing many thoughts with sepa-

rate goals that may even conflict with each other from moment to moment.

Rather than feeling in command of our mind, we may feel that it is like a giant repository for emotional garbage. We may feel we are taking in all sorts of thoughts, attitudes, and judgments, over which we have little or no control. We may even feel that we are victims, always being bombarded by information from the outside world, which results in feelings of fear, conflict, helplessness, and depression.

We may want our minds to feel orderly and free, but so much of the time they seem to be in disorder, burdened, conflicted, unloving, and imprisoned.

Most of us could be much more acutely aware of how often we have negative thoughts. When we truly listen to our own conversations, we may be surprised to discover how often the things we say are negative communications, made up of critical judgments of others or ourselves. There are so many temptations to appoint ourselves as judges, expressing our intolerance for other people's behavior, judging ourselves or other people as inadequate, helpless, unloving, and unlovable.

How can we have loving relationships in our lives when our minds are filled with negative thoughts? Athough it often seems that these negative thoughts have just appeared in the mind by accident, or because of something that someone "out there" has done, the truth is that we have put them there ourselves.

Our egos want us to believe that we are just innocent bystanders, or perhaps even victims, and that our negative thoughts are caused by all the horrible things that have happened to us in our lives. The truth is that the negative experiences that lie in the past no longer exist except in our minds. If we are victims, we are only victims of our own thoughts and judgments, and each of us has the power to free ourselves from them.

Perhaps one of the greatest gifts we have received as human beings is our free will to choose the thoughts we put into our minds. When we finally see our negative thoughts as limited perceptions resulting from our own projections, we can choose to let loving thoughts replace negative ones. When we make this choice, we reaffirm the state of love and happiness that has always been within us, gently guiding us, once again, to freely give and freely receive love. It prepares us for creating the loving relationships that we so desire and deserve.

The Fallacy of the Victim Role

Most of us know only too well what it is like to be rejected in a relationship that has been very important to us. When this happens we often feel like victims. We feel that we have been wronged, dumped on, and that other people have taken advantage of us. We may start feeling that love is dangerous and potentially hurtful. We can even end up in the depths of despair, feeling miserable, angry, depressed, and afraid to love. The world may seem so very unfair that we are not even sure we want to go on living in it.

Many of us who have found ourselves in victim roles, or who have felt that things are always going wrong in our relationships, have discovered that we felt these things because we had been playing victim roles all our lives. We may have even felt that if we were to survive at all we had to play this role. It really did seem as though our experiences in life were *caused by* everything that was happening around us and that we had little or no choice in the matter.

The ego would have us believe that we are victims of our relationships because at the deepest, core level we don't feel deserving of love. It doesn't want us to know the big secret—

that it is *not* the way that other people treat us that makes us victims. Rather, it is our own thoughts that do this. Our own unloving thoughts about ourselves hurt us. Once again, projection is a mirror and not a fact. We put ourselves in the victim role whenever we deny that the feelings of being a victim actually originate in our own minds.

We often choose relationships that are perfect reflections of the belief that we are not deserving of love. Then we mold and manipulate these relationships to match our inner perceptions. When things go wrong, or when we are rejected, the perception that we are victims once again seems to be supported by "proof" from the external world. The cycle continues as our split minds hide from us the ways we have participated in creating this illusion.

When we are caught in the victim role, we often feel, "What did I do to deserve this?!" We go through life feeling trapped, and we often perceive other people as "out to get us," often not realizing that it is only our own thoughts that imprison us in these ways. Thinking the enemy is in our outer world, we fight to be free, taking on the world and everyone in it, battling our relationships, the Creative Source, and ourselves.

Relationships are destined to be disastrous, or at least unfulfilling, as long as we project our victim roles out onto the world. However, our victim feelings begin to disappear the moment we recognize that these are only projections from our own minds.

We release ourselves from our self-imposed bondage when we take responsibility for our thoughts as well as our actions. When we are willing to recognize that it is we who create negative relationships, we can then recognize that it is we who can also create positive ones. It all begins when we make the choice to give up the victim role.

Letting Go of Guilt and Blame

The way of the ego is anger, fear, guilt, and blame. The way of love is to let go of fear, guilt, and blame and to see no value in anger. Most of us are surprised to discover how many hours of every day we spend being angry and reinforcing guilt and blame in ourselves or others.

Guilt is based on the false belief that either you or the other person deserves to be punished. When we follow this belief, we soon start relating to each other as if we were all here to be judged by one another, to decide who is wrong and who is right, who is innocent and who is guilty. The ego's need for punishment is so great that we may become preoccupied with all the things we've done wrong. A part of us is always thinking that we deserve to be punished and to suffer because of these wrongdoings.

Blame is the main tool we have for triggering this guilt. We try to get other people to change their behavior by blaming them and making them feel guilty, while at the same time fighting to deny our own guilt.

We look outside ourselves for the "cause" of the thoughts and feelings we don't like, even though, surprisingly enough, we are the only ones who can put thoughts and feelings into our minds.

More often than not, we don't even notice it happening. We may begin with very simple thoughts, such as: "I hate the way she dresses. I feel embarrassed going out in public with her." Or, "That is the stupidest driver I've ever seen. It's people like him that make this daily commute to work so aggravating for the rest of us."

We may also have more complex thoughts, such as: "I'll never forgive my parents for the way they treated me when I was a child. If they had only been different, I could have been so much happier." Or, "My ex-husband deserves all the horrible things that are happening to him. At last he is getting back all the pain he caused me."   ♥

Most of us are not fully aware of how much, during each day, we hold onto angry and attacking thoughts. These judgmental thoughts act like boomerangs, coming back to hurt us and make us feel miserable. When we choose to recognize that these thoughts hurt us, then we can see that they have no value and can replace them with loving and forgiving thoughts.

Guilt is the center of our split-mindedness. It separates us from our true identity, which is love. Love and guilt cannot coexist. The ego hides this truth from us and would have us believe that we can attack, blame, make other people feel guilty . . . and love them, all at the same time. Nothing could be further from the truth.

The Game of Guilt

Our ego's attraction to guilt causes us to be fearful of love. Many of us have learned this fear only too well, which is why we find it very difficult, indeed, to experience positive, loving relationships.

The game of guilt and blame is a tempting one to play in every relationship, whether it is personal, professional, or political. If there are any rewards to be found in this game, they are self-punishment and feelings of separation.

The game of guilt usually begins with a fearful state of mind in which we perceive that the other person is attacking us or refusing to give us what we *think* we deserve. Our response, then, is to attack back, defending ourselves, blaming the other person, and trying to make him or her feel that whatever went wrong is his or her fault.

In marriage, for example, the game might begin when the husband feels that his wife is not giving him something that he feels he deserves from her. He gets angry. It is as if he picks up a hot steel ball, filled with guilt and blame. He throws it at her. She catches the ball, adds a little more guilt and blame to it and hurls it back. Each player continues to dip into their individual, archaeological collection of emotional garbage and packs still a little more guilt around the ball. The peculiar thing is that once the game gets rolling, it no longer matters to the players how it all got started. If another person interrupts the game, asking what it's all about, neither person knows how to answer.

Another variation of the game of guilt is like a tug-of-war. Each partner tugs away at the other, trying to pull him or her over an imaginary line that will somehow prove that one person is right and the other is wrong.

The solution to the game of guilt is simple, but difficult for most of us to accept, because the ego finds such great

Letting go of the game of guilt sets us free

value in trying to win. We hold on to guilt because at some deep level it supports the belief that we deserve to suffer. At the point when we become more aware of the purpose guilt serves in our lives, we begin to see the insanity of the split mind and we let go, freeing both ourselves and our partners from the game.

The game of guilt can be stopped the same way we stop a game of tug-of-war: One person simply drops the end of the rope, refusing to play the game any longer because he or she no longer can find any value in it. When this happens, the other person is left all alone, holding only the rope.

When one person is left holding the rope in this way, he or she is faced with the choice of either dropping it and ending the game or looking for someone else who is willing to grab ahold. It is both amazing and unfortunate that so many of us go through life continuing to find new partners to play the game of guilt and blame. Meanwhile, the experience of love continues to elude us.

Letting Go

We recently received a letter from a man whose wife had left him because she believed he was a hopeless alcoholic. She was in love with another man and was filing for a divorce. His letter said:

> I was devastated by this, and for perhaps the first time in my life I began to look inside myself. I started applying the principles of Attitudinal Healing, knowing that I could not experience love while I was still holding on to guilt and blame. Finally, everything began to make sense to me.
>
> I have now stopped drinking all together. It has become very clear to me that I have lived a lot of my life enraged, and that I've developed an unforgiving attitude toward myself and other people. I guess, like

everyone else, that I want love and compassion, and I
do not feel that I am capable of unconditional love or
compassion because of this self-anger and guilt.

Thanks to your help, I now recognize that compassion and understanding are the same. Every one of my
attempts to analyze my life failed because the real problem was that my attitude toward life was flavored by
my lack of true compassion, which came from my anger.

I now pray each morning that my life may be held in
God's hands, giving me courage and strength to stay
sober, and to carry messages of love, forgiveness, and
compassion with me everywhere I go. Each day I give
thanks for the love and support I receive.

We can create positive, loving relationships in our lives
when we start focusing our attention on being love finders
rather than fault finders, resisting all temptations to blame
others or ourselves for the difficulties we experience. To
stop the game of guilt, we need only remind ourselves
that love and guilt cannot coexist. Each of us truly has a
choice to experience one or the other. If we choose guilt,
love is automatically excluded. If we choose love, guilt is
excluded.

Letting go of guilt, anger, and blame and deciding instead
to be a compassionate messenger of love can dramatically
change our lives. It is difficult to go through an entire day
without making judgments, getting angry, and condemning
ourselves or others. But our intention to do so is most
important. It is essential to continue to go in the direction of
peace and love, even when we don't succeed in that goal,
every moment of every day.

Let us take one day at a time, starting each morning with
peace and with the intention of not blaming others or seeking guilt. Today, let us pass along the gift of loving rather
than condemning ourselves and others.

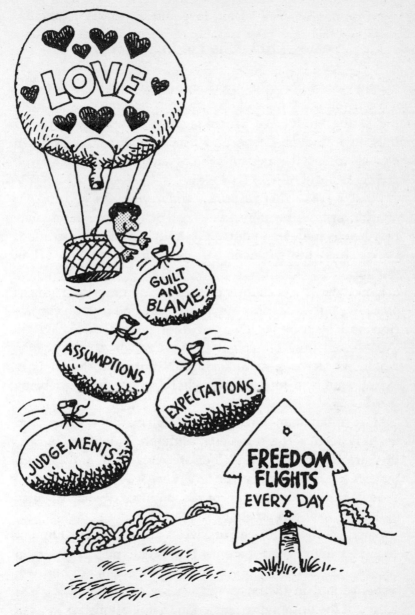

Freedom is letting go of attachments

Seeing Others as Loving or Fearful

Whenever we perceive others around us as being attacking, we can remind ourselves that there is another way of looking at the world. We can remember that there are really only two emotions: love and fear. Knowing this, we can choose to see the person who is attacking us as fearful, giving us a call of help for love.

What is your first response when you feel someone is attacking you? If you're like most of us, your immediate response is to defend yourself or to find some way to attack back. Thus, the game of "attack and defense" is set in motion.

However, if we choose to see the other person not as attacking but as fearful, our hearts can open with compassion and we can be loving to that person. We have all experienced how difficult it is to extend love to someone whom we perceive as attacking us. But how easy it is to extend our love to someone whom we perceive as being fearful.

More often than not, anger, jealousy, depression, and hostility seem to be completely different emotions. In fact, they are all facets of fear. When we view them only as fear, we can see the other person in a new way. We are free to choose a more loving way of responding to what we may initially perceive as an attack on us.

Whenever we perceive ourselves as being attacked by our spouse or lover, child, parents, boss, customer, or a clerk in a store, we can choose to recognize the fear both in our own response and in theirs. When we see that this fear is the source of the underlying tension in that relationship, we can change the way we respond to it. We can stop the game of attack and defense.

We can always choose what we perceive. As we choose to retrain our minds, we can find other ways of perceiving that help us let go of our defenses. We can always choose to see the other person as fearful rather than as attacking. We can respond with compassion and unconditional love rather than anger. Instead of judging the other person, we can come from a place in our hearts where we respond not with fear but with love.

The next time you feel yourself being attacked, stop for a moment and visualize that person with outstretched arms, saying, "Help me." As you use this visualization to remind yourself that the person is actually fearful and giving a call of help for love, you will find yourself responding in an entirely different way. Instead of responding to the perceived attack with your own defense and counterattack, you can find yourself responding to the fearful call for help from a different place within yourself.

3

COMMUNICATING WITH LOVE IN ALL OUR RELATIONSHIPS

Does Anger Bring Me What I Really Want?

Anger is an emotion that many of us experience each day. We seem to accept it as a part of our natural state and actually expect it to be an integral part of life.

As long as we feel that other people cause our anger, we will feel that our anger can be "justified." We will feel that because these other people have actually done things to deserve our wrath and anger, we have to hold on to that anger. As long as we maintain our attachment to this "justified anger," we have little room in our hearts for love. Many people go through their entire lives attached to their justified anger and also wondering why love is passing them by.

It is important to honor our humanness, of which anger is a part. It is also important to become more fully aware of the anger that we are experiencing at any given time and to find positive ways of expressing it. Dumping our anger on other people, or on ourselves, doesn't bring us peace; repressing or suppressing our anger doesn't bring us peace, either. There are better ways to deal with that anger.

Pounding a pillow, shouting in the shower, writing down our thoughts, and carrying on imaginary conversations with the people with whom we feel angry are a few ways of expressing anger without hurting ourselves or others. Then, rather than making an idol of anger, we can ask ourselves, "What purpose does my anger serve? Does anger bring me what I really want? Does it bring me inner peace?"

The subconscious mind has its own law: It will react the same way to a little anger as it will to a lot of it. An angry mind can never be peaceful since it is filled with "attack thoughts." Peaceful and loving thoughts cannot coexist with angry, attacking thoughts.

When we begin to see that it is our own thoughts that are creating the outside world we are experiencing, we begin to see that it is only our own thoughts that we need to change. We can then say with certainty that "My own mind is the one area in the world that I have the ability to alter and control."

The more we choose peace of mind as our only goal, the more we realize that anger never brings us what we want.

Does Attacking Others Bring Me Peace and Love?

We can never achieve peace of mind and love as long as we are attacking other people. This is true no matter how much justification we may find for our anger.

There is a part of us that doesn't want us to be aware that when we are defending ourselves we are actually attacking others, and that attack thoughts and love cannot be experienced simultaneously.

When we attack others, we are unconsciously hiding our own feelings of fear and guilt, which cause us to feel vulnerable in the first place. We then project out onto the other person the emotions that we had inside us, and we deny that these emotions were our own creations. We make the other person our enemy rather than seeing that we ourselves created them as the enemy.

Feeding myself with anger and fear weighs me down

The fallacy of attack and defend is that we think we can be safe as a result of it. Because we feel we're being attacked, we feel vulnerable and weak. If we continue to choose these feelings, we create an endless cycle of defending ourselves and attacking back. We begin to break this cycle when we start to see attacks for what they really are: fearful calls for help.

How can we stop the battle and create peace of mind? By remembering that we can only truly be safe when we have no attack and defense thoughts. We find safety when we remember that we are vulnerable to attack only when we project our own attacking thoughts out onto the world.

As we learn to see our adversaries as fearful and giving us a call for help rather than as attacking us we shift into a position of power. We finally grasp the truth that we each have the ability to choose peace.

When we live one moment at a time, as if it is the only moment there ever was or will be, we begin to see the value of choosing to experience love and peace. Consequently, our attack and defense strategies lose both their appeal and their relevance in our lives. When we live this instant as if it is the only time there is, the ego recedes into the background and the spirit of love reappears.

Listening

We begin to truly establish loving relationships when we commit ourselves to listening with love, tenderness, receptivity, and understanding in all of our communications. We feel our interconnectedness in all our relationships when we listen with a gentle and patient energy that says, "I have all the time in the world to listen to you. You are important to me, and what you have to say is important to me."

Listening with love does not necessarily mean that we have to agree, but it does mean listening without attacking or being defensive. It means listening with no assumptions, no expectations, and no demands. It means listening with an open heart and with respect for the other person as an equal.

Listening doesn't just happen. Rather, it involves a choice, a decision. When we listen to the voice of the ego, we are tempted to not listen to anything else. When we listen to the inner voice of love, we will make the decision to listen with love.

Talking too much, not listening, and constantly interrupting other people before they have finished what they want to say are some of the more common traits of listening to the ego. The underlying message we send to the other person is: "I want you to listen to me because what I have to say is most important." Or, "I am too busy and absorbed in myself to listen to your irrelevant words!"

One of the reasons that so many conflicts occur between parents and children is that we have forgotten how to listen to each other with love and patience. Children learn this easily when it is taught and demonstrated by their parents.

There are some families where children are punished or yelled at simply because they took the risk of sharing how they felt. Often children are not listened to because their parents simply may not be around or, if they are, Dad is too busy reading the paper or Mom is too busy talking on the phone.

Listening doesn't necessarily mean agreement. Listening with love doesn't mean we don't say *no* and set limits for our children or even the adults in our relationships. It does mean, however, giving our children, friends, coworkers, partners, spouses—virtually everyone we meet—the time and space to be heard, not for just the words but for the emotions that need to be expressed.

If there is a single skill necessary for establishing loving relationships, it is the art of listening. So many people, ourselves included, have such busy daily schedules that we often find it easy to tell ourselves that we can't take time to listen.

One way that helps us learn to listen to others is to set aside some time each day to quiet our minds, listen to our own thoughts, and then open ourselves to others. You may find that you can do this best very early in the morning, taking a few moments to enjoy the specific music of a new day. Or you may find that you can do this best very late in the evening, when the house is quiet.

A young man by the name of Tinman Walker has been an important teacher for all of us who have known him at the Center for Attitudinal Healing. When he first came to the center, he was about fourteen years old. Two years before that, he had been hit by a truck while riding his bicycle. Following the accident, he was in a coma for more than eighty days.

When we met Tinman, he had worked very hard in physical therapy to recover from his injuries, but he still had spastic paralysis and a speech impediment. He talked very slowly, and it was often very difficult to understand him.

We remember Tinman's first meeting at the center, where he joined about fourteen other kids his age who faced life-threatening illnesses. Tinman announced that he wanted to tell a joke. Because of his difficulties with speech, a joke that usually took a minute or two to tell took Tinman ten or fifteen.

What followed was a most remarkable thing. As Tinman started telling his joke, everyone—and we mean everyone—listened with their full attention. They focused on every word. There was no impatience. There was no lack of attention. No one's mind wandered and no one tried to interrupt him to tell their own story or to try to finish his for him. While we watched and listened, tears came to our eyes as we recognized the caring and love and patience that everyone was expressing in that room.

When Tinman finally delivered his punch line, the room

filled with laughter. Tinman's face lit up with joy. He went on to say that he had always had a good sense of humor. But since the accident, no one seemed able to take the time to listen to his jokes because it took him such a terribly long time to get them all out. This was the first time anyone seemed to have the patience to let him finish a joke. He added, with tears in his eyes, that he had never before experienced so much unconditional love.

We have a small wooden sign at the center that one of the children gave us. It states, very simply, that "Love is listening, and listening is love." We believe that almost everyone needs a reminder to listen without criticizing or condemning, and that this is the very foundation of all loving relationships.

We have learned from these young people that to have loving relationships we need to learn the art of listening with tenderness. We need to demonstrate, with words as well as with attentiveness and silence, that we have the same interest in others as we have in ourselves.

I am determined to really listen with love and patience

Relationships improve and begin to be healed when we start each day with a goal to become more attentive listeners, people who shower the world with their ability to listen with unconditional love.

We can all learn so much about love by listening to the inner music of silence in quiet moments alone. The Heart of Love that created us all is always there in the silence, reminding us that we are not alone.

Is My Communication in This Relationship for Joining or Separation?

When communicating with others, we rarely ask a most important, though simple, question: "What is the purpose of this communication? Is it for joining or is it for separation, and which do I want to achieve?"

Is the purpose of everything I think, say, and do in all of my relationships really aimed at joining with others? When each of us can answer this question with a definite *yes*, we will experience peace of mind beyond our fondest imaginings. When we decide to make joining our purpose in all our communications, we can begin to experience positive relationships regardless of the person we're with because we have made a decision to extend ourselves in love.

Yet it is so easy to follow the ego, which tells us that the purpose of all communications is to create separation. Like the ego's puppets, we too often dump the anger we feel toward ourselves onto others. We ask provocative questions that put other people on the defensive. We become fault finders, endlessly judging other people's thoughts and actions throughout the day.

The ego can be a very powerful influence in our lives. If we just blindly obey it, we live our lives in a fearful state, guarded, suspicious, and distrusting. We become quick to attack and defend our positions, no matter what they might be.

Sometimes, looking out at the world, we see a place where attacking seems to be the only way people are relating to each other, and separation seems to be the only goal. To the ego it seems like common sense that if you want to survive in such a world, you also must attack and be ready to defend yourself every second of the day. Those are the times when the temptation to obey the ego is the strongest.

It is very important to note here, however, that having the goal of joining rather than separation does not mean we have to agree with the other person or give up our own beliefs. On the contrary, joining is not to be mistaken for "peace at any price!" When we choose joining as the goal of all our communications, we are choosing love as our means of expressing any and all of our thoughts. As we let go of our need to judge other people, or make them wrong, we automatically call upon our own loving energy, which provides us with the most positive and effective expression of our ideas possible. The results are so often highly effective, in every way because we have not wasted our personal resources on games of attack and defense, which do not lead to constructive communication.

At our Center for Attitudinal Healing we begin and end all of our meetings by holding hands, closing our eyes, and reminding ourselves that our single goal is peace of mind and that our purpose in being with each other is to experience joining.

For a long time we encouraged the board of directors to start their meetings the same way, but it was felt that since many of the people on the board were businessmen and women, they would be uncomfortable doing this. Then, about two years ago, a decision was made to start and end all board meetings that way. Since then, there has been less friction and much more peace in our meetings and, in addition, we find that much more is accomplished.

To be joined in hearts and minds, to feel spiritually at one with each other, is the very opposite of what the ego desires for us. We each have a spiritual essence that sees us as joined with the spiritual essence of all others. To attack or hurt another person would be like hurting ourselves. The truth is that we are already joined in spirit. The separation we feel is only an illusion created by our attacking thoughts, supported by the belief that we must always defend ourselves.

We would like to suggest that for the remainder of this day you might ask yourself the following questions in each of your communications: "What is the purpose of this communication? What is it for? Is my goal to join with others, or is my goal to create separation, making the other person wrong and myself right?"

When you choose joining as your goal, you will be choosing happiness, and you will be choosing to bring peace into all of your relationships.

Relationships are for joining

4

FROM RELATIONSHIPS OF CONTROL TO RELATIONSHIPS OF FREEDOM

Having Others Fit into My Mold

Relationships do not work when we allow ourselves to be guided by our egos, which would like to deceive us into believing that other people were put here on Earth so that we might act like gods and mold them into the people we want them to be. The ego is so arrogant that it believes it knows the best shapes for bodies to take, what people should say, what they should do, and how they should do it.

The ego is so arrogant that it will even try to convince us that we actually have the right, or even the duty, to "own" other people's bodies and personalities, dictating how they should live their lives. It deludes us into acting as if we knew exactly the right way to do everything and that our purpose in life is to criticize and tell other people how to live.

As long as we follow this path, we will seek relationships only with people who seem to fit into our mold or who we think we can push into our mold. When the other person doesn't fit, our tendency is to attack, reject, or create a wall of separation that makes him or her our enemy.

The more we try to make others fit our molds, the more we dehumanize them and treat them as objects. We forget names and we feel little or no emotional interaction when we are communicating with them. We may even find thoughts going through our minds such as, "There are certainly a lot of difficult and weird people living in this world! If people were more like me, the world would be a much better place in which to live." We end up communicating with the head rather than with the heart. Our split minds then wonder why we continue to have so much trouble creating loving relationships.

Love flies away when you try to fit others into your mold

Jealousy, Possessiveness, and Competition

Jealousy is an unconscious desire to suffer and to blame other people for our pain. Our ego gives us double messages. On the one hand, it tells us to seek love because our heart is empty, and on the other hand it tells us that we can't trust love because sooner or later we'll be rejected. When we feel jealous, it seems to prove the ego right.

Creating jealousy in relationships is one of the ego's chief functions. We experience jealousy as the hot anger that comes with feeling rejected, often going into rage as the ego desperately tries to control what the other person is doing, even to the point of trying to control his or her physical whereabouts.

Jealousy comes from believing in the ego principles that we should feel guilty about our own thoughts and behavior and that we don't deserve love. We may feel attracted to someone we have seen, even though we're already in a committed relationship. As a way of hiding our guilt, we then deny our own thoughts, quickly projecting them onto our partner. We immediately convince ourselves that our partner is the guilty one, and proceed to grope for more information to prove ourselves right.

The ego may even disguise its jealousy as love, but we all know that jealousy has nothing to do with love. We try to convince other people that we really have their best interests in mind, which may in fact be true. However, there often is another part of us that attempts to control and possess the other person.

Jealousy can destroy a relationship. When we are feeling insecure, jealousy is lurking in the darkness, getting ready to attack. Its influence permeates not just our relationships with our spouses and lovers but also our relationships with coworkers, friends, casual acquaintances, and business associates.

Jealousy may also be found in patronizing relationships between parent and child. The hidden agenda may be: "I really want you to be very successful in all your endeavors, but not more successful than me!" Unconsciously, such a parent is very possessive, holding on to the child tighter and tighter, trying to control or even squash the young person's growth and independence.

The ego wants to possess things and people, and it is never satisfied. No matter what it gets, it is never enough, and because love is missing, it frequently becomes bored with its possessions.

We may become so possessive of the person who is the target of our jealousy that we insist that we know where that person is every moment of the day. The ego disguises this possessiveness as love. It wants to hold on to the other person for dear life. Freedom, individuality, and independence are simply not in the ego's vocabulary.

Our lack of self-confidence may drive us to seek our sense of self-worth outside ourselves. This is often expressed in competition. When we perform better than another person, we may feel good about ourselves—momentarily. When another performs better than we do, we may feel jealous because it triggers our own lack of self-worth. We can actually make our sense of self be dependent on perceiving another person as being less than we are, and in this way we make ourselves the victims of other people's actions.

Competition and jealousy enter many relationships. Both partners may have a low sense of self-worth, and they compete with each other to feel good about themselves. When one person feels good after winning a conscious or unconscious competition with the other, the other person feels down. As long as the couple sees value in playing this game, the relationship stays together even though it may be rocky or troubled.

When one of the partners gains self-confidence and a sense of self-worth, a change may begin to take place in the relationship. The person who is truly self-confident no longer needs to play the competitive game to feel good, and the person who still depends on the competition to feel good is left behind, to play the game all alone or to find someone new to play it with. At this point many relationships go awry.

One way this shows up in relationships is when one of the two partners feels competitive about their careers. One partner attains a new level of personal and professional freedom, and the other person becomes frightened, feeling he or she is going to get left behind, unable to "catch up."

In today's society, where more and more women have successful careers outside the home, the man may feel extremely threatened if the relationship is a competitive one. Because of his own ego problems, he may feel that his

Love knows no competition

professional and financial supremacy are at stake. If he is seeking his self-worth via competition, his jealousy may become very strong, and he may become more and more possessive of his wife, trying to control her as a way to feel better about himself.

Although he may overtly be supportive of his wife in her success, a covert part of him, his ego, is telling him he can't be happy as long as she is more successful than he. His ego tells him that he must either take some of her success away from her or become more successful than she if he is to survive and "win the game."

Jealousy, possessiveness, and competition are, in the truest sense, never about the other person. They are reflections of our own fears and insecurities, projected outward into the world.

When we commit ourselves to love unconditionally, to let go of being a fault finder and interpreting the behavior of others, we begin having the same interest in others as we have in ourselves. Then jealousy and possessiveness begin to fade, becoming less and less an influence in our lives.

Commitment

How can the same word that brings so much joy, security, fulfillment, and continuity to one person engender anxiety attacks, revulsion, and the highest level of fear in another? Since what we see and perceive is what we project from our own mind, perhaps the power that the word *commitment* holds over us is a direct reflection of our own experience with relationships and relating in general.

To commit is to connect oneself in a trusting way with another person or persons, a cause, an ideal, or a purpose. It is to give of yourself, to pledge allegiance to someone or something. A commitment involves giving of your time, energy, talents, and/or emotions to someone or something specific. Used in this context, it is most commonly thought of as a voluntary act by the one making the commitment.

At the opposite pole, commitment can also refer to the consignment of a person to prison or to a restrictive institution. This is almost always an involuntary act in which the person involved is not *making a commitment* but is *being committed* by another person. In other words, the commitment is not the committed person's choice.

Looking at commitments from these extreme perspectives, it is no wonder that many of us are confused about this subject. In relationships we may subconsciously ask the question, "Am I voluntarily entering into this arrangement or am I being coerced, manipulated, or forced into something that I would not otherwise choose for myself?"

Perhaps the confusion arises from the fact that we confuse commitment with a relinquishment of personal power. When we make a commitment we are trusting another person with a part of ourselves. When we are fearful, our egos may try to convince us that we have made a mistake in doing this and that the other person can now control our lives. Even in the most loving of situations, this fear of being controlled can permeate our view of the future.

One of the problems we have with making commitments is that most of us feel guilty because we have failed to fulfill previous commitments we have made. The emphasis on new commitments needs to be on the present, rather than the future; true commitment is renewed each moment of each day. As we renew our commitments in this way, from moment to moment in the present, the present blends with the future to become one, and we find that our commitment is complete.

Commitment is really an all-or-nothing word. We either commit totally or not at all. It doesn't work to just "sort of" commit.

Committing ourselves to love and to following our Inner Teacher is perhaps the highest commitment we can make. As we make peace of mind our only goal, we find ourselves succeeding because our commitments don't depend on anyone or anything else. We can therefore look upon all other things we want to accomplish as our "intentions." There are no *conditions* on our commitment. When our commitment is to accept the unconditional love of the Source that created us, and to give that love to all others we meet, there is no more room for questions or doubts.

Letting Go of Our Scripts for Others

In the privacy of our own minds, each of us is continuously writing scripts for ourselves, those around us, and the world in general. Think about it for a moment. Our scripts have a wide range of subjects: "What should I do today? What should I be doing a year from now? How should I have acted in that situation? My partner or spouse should do such and such in such and such a way. And how about the way the world is going? If I were in charge, I would certainly run it differently!"

The scripts we write in our minds are actually the source of much disappointment, depression, and disillusion in our relationships. We think the scripts in our minds will make us feel "right," or safe, or loved, or just "good," but more often than not they only succeed in creating separation.

Often, without consciously realizing it, we are cajoling or manipulating others, trying to get them to live the scripts we have created for them. Love flies away when we do this; we superimpose our scripts upon the other person, distorting who they really are. Therefore, we rarely, if ever, see others as they truly are, and this causes separation. In the process of trying to make them fit our scripts, we don't hear or see who they really are. We see only what we want them to be.

The scripts we create are so subtle that we hardly recognize they are there. They can easily be identified, however, by the fact that our thoughts are filled with "coulds," "woulds," "shoulds," and lots of "if onlys." Our relationships remain unhealed as we continue to project feelings of judgment, control, lack of confidence, and inadequacy onto others by either silently or verbally inferring that we know what is best. Relationships begin to heal when we consciously decide to tear up our scripts for both ourselves and others.

How do we make the shift from being scriptwriters to honoring and accepting others as they really are? We do this by looking at the part we play in creating these scripts; we can do this by paying attention to words such as "should," "could," "if only," etc. These words tell us that we are superimposing our own scripts over another person, creating separation. We can then begin detaching from our scripts by no longer finding value in them.

Letting Go of Assumptions and Expectations

Most of us consider it perfectly normal to have certain expectations of and assumptions about the people in our lives. But no matter how justified these expectations and assumptions may seem, they can create much conflict.

The ego loves to have us make these assumptions. It knows that in making them, we hand over our power to another person. In effect, we are saying, "I will be happy and peaceful if this other person meets my expectations, and I will be greatly distressed if he or she does not." Since it is impossible to completely control other people, we are bound to be disappointed in our expectations from time to time.

Often, in even our closest relationships, we make love dependent on how well we meet each other's expectations. Although we don't consciously say it, the underlying message is: "If you meet my expectations, I will love you, and if you don't meet them, I will hate you." By the same token, we may feel that if the other person meets our expectations, it is proof that he or she loves us, and if that person doesn't meet them it is proof that he or she either doesn't like us or hates us.

Simply put, the more we assume and expect, the less chance we have of being peaceful and happy.

In marriages, the most mundane things can become critical issues and the source of major family arguments. For example, all hell might break out if a wife forgets to take her husband's shirts to the laundry, or if a husband forgets to get the brakes fixed on his wife's car. And, of course, there's the old story of how leaving the cap off the toothpaste triggers an argument that leads to talk of divorce.

How can we get ourselves off this merry-go-round of frustration and disappointment caused by assumptions and expectations in our relationships? The solution is found in making peace of mind the only goal in our relationships and to not allow that inner tranquillity to become dependent on what another person may or may not do. It is found in placing no value on our assumptions and expectations.

We have seen many relationships begin to thrive and grow the minute the husband made the decision to take responsibility for getting his own shirts to the laundry, or the wife made the decision to take her own car to the garage for repairs. By taking responsibility for their own needs in this way, they suddenly were free of the resentment and bitterness they projected onto the other person.

The more we practice unconditional love and acceptance, the more we discover that our peace of mind need not be dependent on other people's actions. Unconditional love begins by freeing each other from our assumptions and expectations of each other, a decision that almost immediately establishes an infinitely more loving, peaceful, and harmonious relationship. This leaves room in the relationship for us to do what we do out of love instead of obligation.

Letting Go of Controlling Other People

The ego believes that we can find security in our relationships only by controlling other people. As a matter of fact, it thinks that the purpose of relationships is to have someone to control. When we're feeling possessive of another person, or when we are acting as if we own them, we are only responding to the ego's belief that we can find security by controlling other people.

Three of the most common ways our egos attempt to control and manipulate other people are through money, sex, and guilt.

The person in control of the money in a relationship may feel that because he or she is paying the bills, the other person "owes" it to him or her to "make them happy." And the person who has no money may feel that he or she must try to do just that, in trade for financial security.

Although sex is one expression of love in a relationship, it can also be a way of manipulating and controlling the other person. Like money, it can be used as a way to get the other person to do something or give something that he or she may or may not want to give or do.

The ego may also use guilt and blame to control the other person in a relationship. It is one of the most common ways that parents try to control their children. When problems occur in relationships, the ego's first line of defense is to prove the other person at fault. It wants to pile up evidence that the other person has done horrible things, and since the ego is owned by the "guilty" person, he or she must change or the relationship can never improve.

In this game of guilt and blame, the ego believes that the least-guilty person should have the right to control the one who is the most guilty. In relationships that are based on this belief, the struggle over guilt and blame can become the main activity, creating more and more fear and separation, and making it more and more difficult for either person to experience love.

The ego's need to control, its need to manipulate, its desire to possess, or "own," other people, all stem from fear, and this fear always separates us from love. The ego finds a false sense of power or momentary gratification when it feels it has gained control of another person. Even though this sense of power never lasts, the ego continues to deny that true power is only found in love.

We can never truly control other people. Although we may manipulate them into giving us something or doing something we wish, we are also creating a relationship based on fear and separation. As we imprison others with our efforts to keep them under our control, we end up imprisoning ourselves.

We set ourselves free the moment we stop obeying the ego when it tries to tell us that we can only find security in control and possessiveness. The more we allow ourselves to stop trying to control others, the more love we will experience for ourselves, and the more we will discover new opportunities for creating loving, harmonious relationships.

5

FINDING PEACE, LOVE, AND HAPPINESS WITHIN OURSELVES

Stuck in the Past

Have you ever found yourself in a very peaceful situation, such as driving in your car on a beautiful day or taking a walk by yourself, when all of a sudden you felt agitated or upset and you couldn't figure out why? When this happens, it usually means that your mind has slipped back into a moment in the past, to a time of unresolved business. It is as if that old battle is a brand-new one, happening all over again in the present.

Our past perceptions become our current projections as we leave our focus on the present and slip into the past pain and fear surrounding an issue that is still unresolved. We rarely realize at the moment that we are doing this, and the awful, negative past seems to be happening right now. In reality being in the present is something we can all cope with. Think about it! Have you ever *not survived* the present?

Both our minds and our relationships become hostages to the past as we project the pain and conflict of old situations onto the present. Until we are fully awake in the present, our relationships can be overshadowed by the dark clouds of unresolved yesterdays.

Whenever we find ourselves upset, we can almost guarantee that the real source of the conflict will prove to be either in our pasts or in our fears about the future, but definitely not in the present. The unconscious mind has ways of convincing us that our present upset is all in the present and has nothing to do with the past.

Remember that even what happened five or ten minutes ago is now in the past. Whenever you find yourself not feeling peaceful, stop at that moment and ask yourself the question, "Is what I am upset about happening now or is it pain from the past? Am I now projecting my own fears onto the future?"

The mind plays old tapes over and over again. Old dramas get repeated, and our lives start looking like a series of reruns. The split mind hides the truth from us—that the source of our conflict is our unfinished business from past

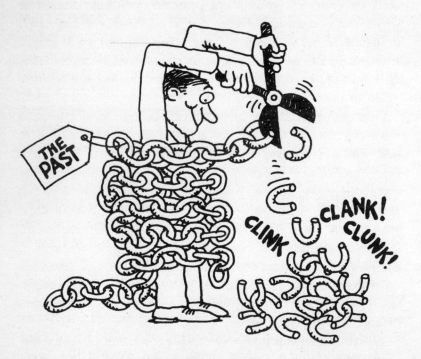

Unchain yourself from the past

relationships, and the past has nothing to do with the present.

It can be extremely helpful if each day we recognize and choose to resolve our unfinished business from past relationships, so that we will be free to live in the present.

Fear of Love and Intimacy

It is difficult to believe that we could be afraid of the very thing that we most crave. But for so many of us our greatest fear is the fear of love and intimacy. Often this is because we have been hurt in the past and feel that we must do everything we can to avoid getting hurt again. We frequently end up feeling unlovable and, out of fear of rejection, we may even create an attitude of aloofness that keeps people away so that we don't have to take the risk of being rejected.

When we are feeling alone and without intimate relationships, we may become convinced that the whole world is a very unfair place. These feelings can become particularly intense whenever we see other people hugging, kissing, and being close. As our resentment or anger builds up, we may send out negative messages that can further keep people away. Sometimes, even though we don't intend it, the energy we create around us says, "Stay away!" even though we feel that we want closeness and intimacy.

For many of us, the fear of intimacy started in childhood. We may have felt that we did not measure up to our parents' or teachers' perceptions and expectations of what we should be or how we should perform. We began making judgments about ourselves, feeling that we did not "perform" as well as other people wished us to.

Many of our childhood experiences are still stored in our

memory bank, telling us that we will only be loved according to how well we perform. Because we may be fearful that we are going to be judged negatively, we become afraid to take the risk of social interchange. We may feel that we will be at a loss for words or, because of our own feelings of inadequacy, we may not want to become too involved with other people because we are fearful that sooner or later it will lead to sexual relations and our performance might be judged negatively.

Many of us have difficulty trusting because we shared our innermost secrets with someone in the past who later used this knowledge against us. So we are fearful of intimacy, afraid to take the chance of sharing our deepest feelings again.

This is particularly true for men who as children did not have male role models who were willing to share their feelings. Too often they observed that sharing their feelings was falsely interpreted as being weak. So the idea of sharing their innermost feelings with others makes them fearful of rejection. This often is expressed by the ego's voice saying, "If people find out who you really are, they will most certainly reject you."

Another way of looking at intimacy is "into-me-see." But the part of us that is afraid of being rejected creates a disguise to prevent other people from seeing in. We become convinced that if we don't protect ourselves in this way people will discover who we really are and they will reject us. We all want intimacy and closeness, yet our attachment to fear shields us from the very thing we most desire.

To have this intimacy, we need to see no value in fear and guilt, and we need to let go of our attachments to these illusions. Our fear comes from our own perceptions that we are guilty of doing terrible things in the past and that we deserve to be rejected. These perceptions create within us the belief that we don't deserve love. We then project this

We need to trust love not fear it

belief out onto the world and we get back exactly what we project, ending up with the feeling that we are victims of our relationships.

The ego will do everything it can to make us afraid of love and to block us from forgiving ourselves, loving ourselves, accepting love, and giving love to others.

We need to trust in love, not fear. Forgiving ourselves and others is the first step for letting go of our fear of rejection and fear of love and intimacy.

Trust

Working with thousands of people who have relationship problems, we have found that the number-one complaint is the lack of trust in the other person. Hiding the facts of our lives from each other, about money, infidelity, etc., is sure to put any relationship in jeopardy.

Mistrust does not come about only because of the behavior of the other person in the relationship. Rather, it stems from projecting our own feelings of self-doubt and mistrust onto the world.

Unless a relationship is based on honesty and trust, it can only go in an endless circle, from one conflict to another. Honesty is having integrity and consistency in all that we think, say, and do.

There is a high incidence of divorce in relationships where there is much mistrust. Even after the breakup, many of these relationships remain unhealed. In all too many divorces, unforgivingness continues for many years, sometimes for a lifetime, affecting the relationships of everyone involved. Where there is unforgivingness from past relationships, new relationships may also be filled with mistrust.

We cannot create positive relationships, ones that are whole and totally loving, until we have healed the unhealed relationships from the past. To learn again how to trust, we need to learn to let go of any emotional investments we still have in our hurtful past.

We can trust in the present only when we have truly forgiven the past. This means letting go of the many perceptions we learned very early in our lives. For instance, it means being willing to stop listening to the voice of the ego, telling us never to forgive or forget old hurts because history will surely repeat itself and we might get hurt again.

Trust means looking beyond the physical body and the disguises people wear. We cannot really trust "bodies" because they come and they go. We can only trust what is changeless, and this means trusting the spiritual essence that is the true identity for each of us. Trust means looking past behavior based on fear; it means choosing to see the light of love and the innocence of a child in the eyes of everyone we know, think about, or meet in our daily lives.

Think of an infant child for a moment. Is there anything this baby could possibly do that you would not forgive, or

I will not be afraid of love today

that would cause you to hold the infant's past behavior against him or her? We think not.

Rather than concentrating on another person's body and its behavior, we can learn to trust in the inherent innocence, the spiritual essence, of every being.

We cannot overemphasize how difficult it is to create positive, loving relationships, ones that are whole and totally loving, until we have healed the mistrust of the past. If we wish to learn how to trust in the present, we have only to let go of our negative perceptions from the past.

Let us base our trust on those truths that are eternal rather than on the hurtful experiences we have had in the past. Let us base our trust on the spiritual essence expressed through each person, rather than on something that we believe they must do in order to earn our love and trust.

Trust is based not on what we see or hear but on what we inherently know or believe to be true. There is a frightened child within each of us that usually expresses itself in the form of the angry, attacking adult. Let us not base our trust on what our eyes tell us about other people's behavior, but let us choose instead to see the shining light of innocence and love as their true identity and our own.

Choosing Happiness

Can happiness really be a choice in a world that often seems so crazy and unfair? The answer is *absolutely!* Happiness is our natural state of mind. It is only our ego that creates the illusion that just the opposite is true. The ego does this by encouraging us to seek happiness outside ourselves, though no matter how hard we try we never seem able to find lasting happiness in the external world.

It can be a rule of thumb that when we find ourselves

Happiness is a choice

unhappy we have chosen the wrong goal. Our unhappiness means that we are following our ego, which has told us that happiness can be found by "getting" something. It might be a new car, a new relationship, a vacation trip, or any of a multitude of things that the external world offers. When we believe, as our ego tells us, that we will find happiness by getting these things, and then we don't get them, it really does feel as if happiness is beyond our reach.

Happiness is a decision and an inner choice and doesn't have to have anything to do with the events that take place in the outer world. Perhaps the highest form of happiness and joy we receive is through the act of giving our love and helping another person on the pathway of life, reminding us once again that to give is to receive.

Our ego thinks happiness is getting something we want, like a bicycle or a car. But happiness that is based on getting, not giving, is not a permanent kind of happiness.

We have seen many people who have chosen happiness even in the face of crises such as losing a job, having a home burn down, having a car stolen, and even in the face of critical illness or losing a loved one. They can choose peace at any moment in their process of experience. This does not mean, however, that they don't experience all the other human emotions. What is different is that they have chosen peace of mind as their only goal, knowing that peace of mind has nothing to do with their external world. They know that happiness is due to the boundless and everlasting love in their hearts and that is something they can never lose.

6

FORGIVENESS AND HEALING

Attachments: The Jailer Within

The ego is always focused on finding substitutes for love. It would have us act like children in a toy store, convinced that our happiness depends on having, only for ourselves, everything within our reach. Furthermore, our egos would have us make idols or gods of the many things in the toy store of life. These false needs that our egos want to convince us are necessary for happiness are what we call "attachments."

What is an attachment? It is a certain way that we use people, situations, and things to actually create barriers against love and our own inner peace. We create attachments any time we set up specific conditions, expectations, or requirements for what must happen, or for what other people must do, or for what we will have to possess in order for us to experience happiness in life.

Most of the time our attachments have definite goals, and when these are not satisfied we are unhappy and anything but peaceful. For example, we may have an attachment to another person performing in a certain way that will benefit us. When that attachment is very important to us, and they don't "come through and deliver" exactly as we wanted them to, we feel like victims, powerless to control our lives. In this way, our attachments become our jailers, binding us with the chains of our expectations.

When we honestly ask ourselves, "What am I attached to?" most of us find that we have many, many attachments indeed. The list might go on and on, including such things as money, sex, drugs, chocolate, being thin, having a fancy car, jewelry, books, or having a beautiful body. We can even become attached to pain, anger, guilt, fear, depression, failure, suffering, the need to always be "right," and even unhappiness itself. Whenever we are not peaceful in our lives, we can usually trace it back to one or more of our attachments.

When we're on a diet, we often give the bathroom scale the power to determine whether we should love ourselves and be happy that day or hate ourselves and feel miserable. Or we give that power to the weather, as when we are planning to have a picnic or play tennis and it rains.

Most of us have a long list of attachments and addictions that we subconsciously use as poor substitutes for love. In our workshops we often ask the people to visualize a garbage can into which they have dumped all their attachments, realizing that they interfere with experiencing love.

All attachments are based on the ego's belief in the scarcity of love and on the illusion that there is an emptiness inside us that needs to be filled up by people or things or events outside us. What the ego doesn't tell us is that its needs can never be satisfied. It is insatiable no matter how much we feed it.

Our attachments keep us from recognizing our spiritual essence and discovering that true happiness is found only by going inward. Our attachments, and the idols we make of them, keep us feeling separate from each other and actually take us further and further from the love and intimacy we seek in life.

Most of us have seen our relationships go down the tubes when we were attached to controlling the other person and having them fulfill our conditions and expectations. The

I become my own jailer when I am attached to guilt

more attached we are to having other people perform according to our expectations, the more we feel like victims, powerless to manage our lives.

The reason why our attachments interfere with our relationships is that they cause us to feel that our happiness and peace of mind depend on forces outside us. It does not matter whether our expectations are happily fulfilled or they fall quite short of what we desired; in either case it will seem that the results were influenced and controlled by people and events outside us. In reality, the most powerful forces influencing love and peace of mind begin, change, and end right in our own minds.

Like a ball and chain, our attachments keep us limited and imprisoned in our own fear. They have us looking around the world for the pot of gold at the end of the rainbow, which presumably is going to bring us love and happiness. All the time, the ego hides the truth from us, that the pot of gold is the abundance of universal love that always resides in our hearts.

We can't always change the world, but we can always

The key to freedom from attachments is changing my mind

change our own minds. We can choose to hold on to our attachments or we can choose to let them go. When we let go of them, we break their bonds, freeing ourselves from our victim roles and awakening to our own ability to choose.

To have loving relationships, it is most helpful to recognize our attachments and no longer find value in making them the condition upon which our love, happiness, and well-being are based.

Do I Want to Be Happy
or
Do I Want to Be Right?

There is a part of us that is so interested in being right that we are quite willing to make other people wrong in order to achieve that goal. The main way we do this is by attacking or blaming other people for difficulties in our lives. Through blame, guilt, and our own "justified anger," we fight every inch of the way to prove that the other person is wrong and we are right. As long as we try to maintain this attachment to being right, we cannot experience happiness, peace of mind, or love.

Most of us have a support system consisting of friends and family members who agree with us and tell us that we are justified in our anger and resentment. These same people may also support us in finding value in being right rather than happy.

Whenever we have attachments to being right, we make condemning judgments on other people or on the world and we turn to our support system to find people who will agree with us. Soon our minds are filled with attacking thoughts and feelings of justified anger, and there is no room in the mind or heart for happiness or love.

If we have relationships that are based on our desire to be
right, and if we tend to hear those who agree with us while
being deaf to the ones who don't, it could be helpful to ask
ourselves these questions: "Is this really bringing me peace
of mind? Is this way of living my life bringing me happiness?" If the answer is no, then we have just discovered a
new opportunity to choose to be happy rather than right
and to bring love rather than feelings of separation into our
relationships.

The Role of Unforgiveness
in Unhealed Relationships

Unforgiveness plays the starring role in every unhealed relationship. From this place of unforgiveness comes judgments
that sound absolutely true. In our minds, a great curtain
goes down, protecting us from seeing our own projections
for the illusions they really are.

The world would have us believe that we are surrounded
by people who do unforgivable things; that because this is
the way the world is, it is both normal and healthy not to
forgive.

An unforgiving mind has its own agenda. It includes
distorting what is real until it is barely recognizable. In the
face of it, we lose sight of our singular desire to have peace
of mind as our only goal. Suddenly our mind is filled with
numerous mixed and conflicting goals. Our unforgiving
thoughts convince us that everything that is unpleasant or
wrong is the other person's fault and that people do unforgivable things for which they must be punished.

Judgments and righteous condemnation are the themes
for the script of unforgivingness, and we alone write that
script. No one else has the capacity to write our prejudices

and judgments into our relationships except ourselves, just as no one else has the ability to choose forgiveness.

When we choose to keep a relationship unhealed, we also choose unforgivingness. Likewise, forgiveness is the only means by which we heal a relationship.

Since the way we experience a relationship is primarily through our projected thoughts and feelings, it is our own condemning thoughts that injure us, and it is our own forgiving thoughts that will set us free.

Forgiving the Unforgivable

Belief in the Unforgivable

The ego believes that some of the things people do are simply unforgivable. It believes that when someone does something unforgivable we must hold onto our anger toward that person and our hurts and never forget them. Falsely, it tries to warn us that to be unforgiving is a way to protect ourselves from being hurt again when really the opposite is true.

The result of believing in the ego's thought system is that we turn our anger toward others against ourselves, filling our lives with suffering, misery, rejection, and unhappy relationships. The ego fully believes in unpardonable sin and is constantly on the lookout for it.

As long as we believe that our identities are limited only to our body and personality, we will continue to accept the ego's belief system. We will believe that there are people in the world who do things that are unforgivable, and until we can let go of that belief, we will continue to suffer.

As long as our ego convinces us that our interpretation of what our eyes, ears, and other senses tell us is the truth, we will set ourselves up as gods and will become judge and jury deciding who is innocent and who is guilty and who has committed an act that is unforgivable and does not deserve our love.

Mistakes Are Errors to Be Corrected

To find inner peace, which is the enemy of the ego, and to once again experience the reality of love and innocence, we need to go beyond the ego's belief system that people do things that are unforgivable. As long as we hold unforgivable thoughts in our mind, we will not be able to experience total inner peace.

As we turn away from the ego's thought system and go toward the thought system of love, we can remind ourselves of the true reality of innocence in others and in ourselves. There then can be a recognition that it is the ego's belief in unforgivingness that keeps love and peace away from us.

When an assassination attempt was made on Pope John Paul II's life, he went to the man who had seriously wounded him and forgave him face to face. The whole world was deeply moved, and many hearts were opened when he did this, demonstrating that everyone deserves our love and that there is nothing that cannot be forgiven.

We have all done things for which we feel ashamed, and at times there have been things we may have done that we thought were unforgivable. It is helpful to see these things as mistakes to be corrected rather than as unforgivable acts in which we need to be continuously punished. Because of the tenacity of our ego, many of us find forgiving ourselves to be one of the most difficult things to do in life. To create loving relationships, we need to learn how to forgive ourselves as well as others.

Willingness to Forgive

It is essential to remember that we can never forgive others or ourselves through the ego, since it finds true forgiveness intolerable. The ego is the part of the split mind that believes existence is defined by separation. The ego encourages unforgivingness, knowing that it will cause separation and lack of love. Sometimes the ego will encourage false forgiveness, such as telling us to say, "I am a big enough person to put up with her terrible behavior. But I will never forget how she hurt me to my dying day!" This, of course, is anything but forgiveness.

When we have heated anger and resentment in our hearts because of another person's actions, just saying an affirmation of "I forgive you" usually doesn't work. It is impossible for the ego to actually forgive. We can, however, have a *willingness* to forgive. We then can recognize and take our anger, resentment, and unforgiving thoughts and give them to that Higher Power that is always residing in our hearts. Those feelings then can be transformed into love by the spiritual part of our split minds.

Love's way is completely opposite of the ego's thought system. Love tells us that nothing that we do, or that another person does to us, is unforgivable. It believes that we all make mistakes, but that all mistakes are forgivable and can be corrected.

Everything Is a Positive Lesson

How can it possibly be that everything in life is a positive lesson? Nearly every day we hear of horrendous situations that cause us to ask, "Is there really a loving force in the world?" Countries are torn apart with civil strife and war, with families being divided by violence and death. Many people are fighting just to survive disasters such as floods, pollution of the environment, hurricanes, tornadoes, rampant fires, and earthquakes. Others are challenged with the loss of loved ones through life-threatening illnesses such as cancer and AIDS. How is it possible to find positive lessons in all these?

In and of themselves, these experiences are not positive. Yet out of our responses to them there can come many learning experiences that do, in the final analysis, prove to be beneficial. It is often at critical junctures in our lives, where we face what seem to be insurmountable challenges, that we also discover our greatest opportunities for growth. We rise above what we believed were our limitations, discovering that we are stronger, wiser, more compassionate, or more creative than we ever imagined we could be.

Recently, a woman we know lost both of her young children, just one year apart, to unrelated illnesses. Through her desire to heal her own pain, she gave support to other parents facing similar crises. Through her own healing she became extremely sensitive and compassionate. She is now professionally involved at the Center for Attitudinal Healing, in programs for adults and children with life-threatening illnesses.

When we are faced with such challenges, how is it possible to utilize the belief that somewhere in this experience is a benefit, a good, or that it could possibly be perceived as a source of positive growth?

We begin by letting go of the illusion that we are victims, even when it seems that there is a world of evidence to prove otherwise. As soon as we let go of the victim illusion, we automatically begin taking responsibility for our lives and taking charge of the challenges that face us.

Our next step is to remember that what we perceive as the external world is really a reflection of our own inner world, and we begin empowering ourselves to create a positive reality. Our mind becomes more open, and we begin to see that regardless of what occurs in our lives, without exception, we can choose to perceive it as an opportunity for growth. This cannot occur, however, until we fully accept, feel, and honor our full experience of the challenge, since we cannot rise above what we cannot accept.

To have the belief that every experience, without exception, is a positive lesson in our lives, from which we can learn and grow, itself generates our willingness to receive all of life's experiences. We can then create positive results from all that life offers us, accepting each lesson with gratitude even before we know what the benefits might be. While our willingness opens us up to the opportunity for growth, our gratitude opens us up to receiving it.

THE WAY HOME

From Special to Holy Relationships

Holy Relationships

Holy relationships are based on the laws of love rather than the laws of the ego. They are relationships where two minds are joined as one, with the shared intention of living by the principles of giving, joining, and forgiving, and where both wills become one with God.

In holy relationships, both people see the light of love in themselves, each other, and in other people equally. Their lives are based on the belief that our natural state is one of love, and there can never be any scarcity of love.

In holy relationships, there is a willingness to live without attempting to control, manipulate, dominate, demand, or possess any other person. It is a relationship where trust and equality replace selfishness, jealousy, competition, attack, and defense. It is a relationship where each person's growth, individuality, and independence are fully supported, and where both people are filled with the fire of compassion for this planet, this universe, and for all that life is.

It is a relationship where there is only unconditional love, where two souls come together as one, bringing light and healing to the world around them. It is a relationship where interest in the other person's welfare is equal to interest in oneself. It is a relationship based on unconditional love and forgiveness, excluding no one from that love.

Special Relationships

In this book we refer to "special relationships" as ones that specifically serve the ego. They are based on conditional love and a belief in separation. They are often love–hate relationships that keep us quite separate from each other and our Creative Source. They serve the ego's judgment that some people are more deserving of our love than others. They are relationships where one person is loved more than any other, and they are relationships from which all others are excluded.

Some of the principles that characterize "special relationships" are:

1. A feeling that love is scarce
2. Fear and separation anxieties
3. Attack and defense
4. Exclusiveness
5. Alternating between love and hate
6. Getting rather than giving
7. Conditional love
8. Illusions of love
9. Possessiveness
10. Jealousy
11. Lack of equality
12. Manipulation
13. Competition
14. Desire to change and control others
15. One's selfish interests come first
16. Need to suffer
17. Fear of God
18. Fear of loneliness
19. Attachment to the physical body
20. Demanding attitude toward others
21. Denial of one's spiritual essence

Our ego sets up love–hate relationships to make us afraid of love and thus to keep us from discovering it. By following the ego's belief system, the presence of God, the presence of love, evades us, and we are invaded by chaos, conflict, frustration, righteous anger, and unhappiness.

A holy relationship is a total commitment to the Creative Love Force manifested through our expression of unconditional love.

The Inner Teacher

Have you ever made a decision based on what other people say is correct, even though "something" inside you told you it should be otherwise? Then, when the results of that decision didn't work out, you stated with adamant regret, "I *knew* I should have followed my *instincts*!" This instinctive awareness, which emanates from beyond the five senses, can be identified as the Inner Teacher. This Inner Teacher is a personal guidance system that is completely individualized. Everyone in the world has such a guidance system, and it offers each of us everything we need to know.

There are many teachers that come into each of our lives. Some influence us at close range and over long periods of time, such as parents, relatives, and friends, while others touch our lives only briefly, though they may leave lasting impressions.

Heroes and role models in sports, the sciences, the arts, medicine, education, entertainment, and the like, help us to shape our values, commitments, and ultimately our experiences, patterning the blueprints of our lives. Although the lessons they offer vary in content as well as degree of influence, each, in its unique way, has in common the fact that it is external, that is, it emanates from a source outside oneself. We are, therefore, recipients of the lessons, actions, and accomplishments of others, which we digest and assimilate into our own experience.

Your Inner Teacher, however, differs considerably from all others, in that it is not in any way affected by exterior forces. Without exception, your Inner Teacher always has your own best interests at heart. Unique to you, it emanates from your inner source, that is, your spiritual self. It is an intuitive way of knowing what is best for your own learning and growth, and it manifests itself in a variety of forms.

Some of us recognize the messages from our Inner Teachers as a "hunch," while for others it is "a gut feeling." Still other people see it as a red light/green light, or perhaps a neon sign, in their mind. Some actually hear an "inner voice" or have what could be called "inner dictation," silent words being dictated in their mind. Since words and form are so often used to separate us, we can honor the fact that each person communicates with his or her Inner Teacher in the way that is individually appropriate.

Listening to our Inner Teacher, or Inner Guide, is really a way of listening to our heart, which guides us along a path of having positive, loving relationships. Decisions that are made by listening to this inner guidance have a totally different outcome than listening to the voice of the ego in our head, with all of its judgments and negative thoughts from the past.

In order to tap into this Inner Teacher, we need only to express a little willingness to listen to what it tells us. The simplest way to learn to hear this inner voice is to come to the moment with empty, open hands holding on to nothing from the past.

We can then be still and ask for guidance, knowing that the counsel of our Inner Teacher comes from love, helping us to decide what we should think, say, and do. Doing this takes trust and a willingness to act upon what we "hear." This experience expands and deepens our relationship with our Inner Teacher and with each other.

DAILY LESSONS FOR THE TRANSFORMATION OF FEAR INTO LOVE

Love and guilt cannot coexist,
and to accept one is to deny the other.

INTRODUCTION

The purpose of the lessons that follow is to help bring Attitudinal Healing concepts into your daily experience. The emphasis is not on changing other people but on changing only the thoughts in your own mind.

These lessons were designed to give practical help in everyday situations, the kinds of situations that any of us might find ourselves in. You'll be taking the concepts that you are already familiar with from reading the first parts of the book, reviewing them briefly, and then applying them in practical ways to your everyday life.

The goal for each of these daily lessons is inner peace, and the themes at the core of each lesson are forgiveness and unconditional love. Don't worry if, upon your first reading, you find a concept difficult to accept, or you just can't see how a particular lesson is relevant in your life at this time.

Uncertainties and questions are a natural part of the process. Just keep in mind that these doubts will pass without exception, as you practice the lessons. The experience that comes from a commitment to practicing these lessons will allow your perceptions to change, and that brings the experience of peace and love into your heart and mind and into your relationships.

Suggestions

The best way to start is to keep this book at your bedside and read one lesson each morning just before rising. Additionally:

1. Each day upon awakening, take a few deep breaths, exhaling slowly each time. Relax and remind yourself that peace of mind is going to be your only goal today.

2. Read your single lesson for the day and then use your imagination to create a mental picture of where and how you see yourself applying that lesson.

3. Write today's lesson on a card or piece of paper and do your best to take just a few seconds to look at it several times throughout the day.

4. If there is someone in your life who would like to join you in these lessons each day, either in person or on the phone, so much the better.

5. Be sure that you apply the day's lessons to everyone and everything in your life, without exception.

6. Before retiring in the evening, be sure to read and reflect on the day's lesson once again.

7. When you have completed all the lessons, your learning will be facilitated if you begin again and repeat the series. Some people also use these lessons as daily reminders or inspirations, helping them to keep moving forward on their path toward peace of mind in all their relationships.

8. As you continue in this way, you will find that you are thinking about the lessons and applying them consistently in your life, even without consciously thinking about them.

THERE IS ANOTHER WAY OF LOOKING AT THE WORLD, AND I AM DETERMINED TO FIND IT

❦

Learn to look upon the world
as a means of healing the separation.

There are times when we look at the problems we face on our planet and everything seems filled with fear and tragedy, doom and gloom. We wake up some mornings wondering what awful things are going to happen next. Events in the outside world not only look dismal but our inner world is filled with depressing thoughts as well. Our egos tell us to look at all this as proof that we are helpless victims living in an unfair, cruel, and unloving world.

But there is another way of looking at the world, and we can find it by learning to shift our perceptions. Our perceptions are determined not by what is happening outside us but by what is happening inside us, by what we think and believe.

Nearly all of us have gone through periods in our relationships when the chaos and despair seemed almost more than we could stand. Then, without any change in the circumstances, we found ourselves breathing a little easier and experiencing more inner peace. It was not the outside events that changed how we felt and changed the world we saw. It was only our thoughts and attitudes that changed. As our inner world changed, we began looking at the world in a different way and, sure enough, we found a different external world.

Perhaps one of the greatest gifts that we have been given in life is the ability to choose the thoughts and beliefs we put into our mind. We really can choose to be free of a world built on the self-imposed bondage of fear.

We can choose to believe in the illusion of a world filled with fear, hate, conflict, and war, or we can choose to believe in a world founded on everlasting love. When we choose the illusory world, we believe that what is outside us is the cause. When we choose the world of love, we believe that our own thoughts are the cause of what we see and experience.

In every situation we find ourselves in, no matter what it might be, we can always make the decision to have peace of mind as our only goal. We can always choose, once again, to see the world differently. As we choose peace of mind, our perceptions change and we reaffirm our commitment to a journey of personal transformation, doing our part to help transform the world we see.

Example

During most of my life, if someone tried to convince me (Jerry) that there was another way of looking at the world, I would have thought he was crazy. I was proud of being a hard-nosed skeptic. To me, only the physical world and my interpretations of it were real. My perceptions were my only reality, and I was convinced that what I saw and experienced was the way things really were.

Mind you, most of my life any kind of continued happiness or peace of mind escaped me, and I was convinced that this was the nature of the world. My perception was that the world is frequently cruel and unloving. I felt that the world did its best to kick me around and I did my fair share of attempting to kick back.

I was like a porcupine who wanted love and couldn't

understand why no one wanted to hug me. My perception was that I had no capacity for love. I saw only a world in which I was unlovable, and so it was impossible to have a positive, loving relationship.

In 1975, I started to learn that when I embraced the world, it embraced me back. I began learning how to take responsibility for my own thoughts and feelings and since then I have done my best to become a "love finder" rather than a "fault finder." I have begun to choose love rather than fear, peace rather than conflict, and to stop blaming others or condemning myself.

There is another way of looking at the world. We can choose to perceive it from our heart rather than our head. The more we let our hearts guide our perceptions of the world, the more we are able to accept that our purpose in life is to love and to forgive, and the more we are able to experience peace, love, and happiness.

If I become upset, frustrated, and angry, I will remind myself that there is another way of looking at the world, and I can choose to see my present upset in this other way.

My ego is like an unhuggable porcupine

ONLY MY OWN THOUGHTS AND ATTITUDES CAN HURT ME

Nothing can hurt you unless you give it the power to do so.

Identifying the Cause

The unpleasant neighbor, the angry store clerk, the bus driver who would not wait, the person we love rejecting us . . . all of these can seem to be the source of so much anger or pain. And yet none of them are really the cause of the hurt we may feel. It is not people or situations outside us that cause our frustration, fear, disappointment, or upset. Rather, only our own thoughts and attitudes about these people or situations are the cause.

Does Justified Anger Bring Me Peace?

When we choose to believe that the outside world is the cause of all we feel, our happiness and peace of mind depend on our ability to change other people so that they will behave in ways we want them to. If things are not going right for us, we start looking for someone to blame. If someone is yelling at us with great anger in his or her voice, and we are sure we have done nothing to deserve this kind of treatment, we may believe that we are victims and have no choice but to feel hurt. Other people's behavior seems to justify our anger, and even our self-righteous rage, and it seems impossible for us to choose peace of mind and love instead of anger.

Again and again and again, let us be reminded that it is not people or events outside us that cause us to be upset; only our own thoughts and attitudes can hurt us.

Example

A few months ago, I (Diane) was consulting with Jerry at San Francisco General Hospital's AIDS program. Parking is usually very difficult there, and I generally plan to arrive a half hour early to find a place to park. On this particular day, I found a parking place right near the front entrance.

The two-hour Attitudinal Healing session at the hospital went quite well. In the lesson that day, we had emphasized that we can always choose peace instead of conflict, and that it is only our own thoughts and attitudes that hurt us.

Following the session, I went to my car only to find a green car parked beside mine and blocking my way. I thought, "Oh, well, this person has just run in for a five-minute errand and is sure to leave in a minute or two."

I waited a few minutes, and a few minutes turned into twenty and twenty turned into forty. I was getting panicked. Maybe the owner of the green car had run in for an eight-hour shift!

I became very upset. I had to be at a meeting across town in half an hour. I'd never make it if the driver of the green car didn't come soon. I noticed that with each person that came even close to the green car, I got angrier and angrier. Then I remembered what we had discussed in the meeting about choosing peace on the inside regardless of what is happening in the external world. And you know what? It made absolutely no difference! I was so sure that I was right that I was the victim of a very inconsiderate person, and quite confident that most people would line up behind me and support me in my belief.

I was really getting angry and outraged. I caught myself and thought, "Diane, you are acting deranged!" I decided to sit there a few minutes and get very quiet. I then said to myself, "I absolutely don't know what's going on here, but there must be something I can learn from all this!"

What came into my mind was the lesson Jerry and I had just spent two hours discussing: "I can choose peace over conflict." Was I a victim or could I choose peace? I said aloud, "Okay, I choose peace." I became very quiet and what emerged from a place deep inside me was that I should ask the next person I saw if he or she knew anything about the green car. A man emerged from the building and I called to him, "Excuse me, but could you tell me anything about this green car?"

"Oh, yes," he said. "Just go around to the front of the building, to the right, through the front door, down the hall, and it's the last office on your right. They'll be able to tell you about the green car." I was amazed.

I went into the building and asked at the office on the right if anyone knew anything about the green car. Simultaneously, two office workers replied, "Oh, yes. Just go down the hall and into the last door on the right and they can tell you about the green car."

By this time I was really fascinated, and I had totally calmed down. I felt very peaceful inside. I knew that I really had no idea of what was going on in the outside world just then. I walked into the office that had been pointed out to me. There was a woman sitting at a desk and a man standing beside it. I said very calmly, "Excuse me, but can you tell me about the green car out there?"

The man standing there said very pleasantly, "Oh, yes, it's my car."

I replied in a calm, gentle voice, "Well, you know the gray car next to the building that your car is blocking? Well, that's mine and I was wondering if you could take a few minutes and move your car so that I could get out."

The woman behind the desk said, "Excuse me, but did you know that's a police tow-away zone you're parked in?"

Peace of mind is a choice

In total shock, and with a very timid voice I replied: "Well, no, I didn't know that!"

"And did you know that we are the police?" the man asked.

I said, "No, I didn't know that, either!"

The man looked at me and smiled. "You know," he said, "We were just saying that when this person who owns the gray car comes storming in here, ranting and raving, we're going to have that car towed away. But you came in so nice that, well, I'll be glad to move my car for you."

As we walked out toward the parking lot together, the man explained, "Several times a day we normally tow cars that have parked there. At the very least, we ticket them. But this time something inside me said to just wait for the person with the gray car. That's why I blocked it in order to see who it was. And I'm glad I did."

"You wouldn't believe what went through my mind," I said. And then I told him the whole story. Before I got into my car, we gave each other a hug and then we went our separate ways. As I drove away, I found myself thinking about what a wonderful lesson this had been. I had been so certain that I was right and felt ironclad in my righteous indignation. I also thought of all the times in my life that I was so sure I was right. It reminded me that when we choose peace instead of conflict, we find the love we are seeking not only within our minds but in the external world as well. Every relationship we encounter becomes one of love.

If I find myself angry about people's behavior, I will remind myself that it is only my own thoughts and attitudes that hurt me.

I AM DETERMINED TO SEE ALL MY PERCEPTIONS AS MIRRORS OF THE THOUGHTS IN MY MIND

❧

It is when judgment ceases
that healing occurs.

Perceptions Mirror Our Inner Selves

Most of the time we hold onto our perceptions of other people as if they were absolute truths and indisputable facts. But have you ever had one of those days when everything seemed to go wrong, when everyone around you seemed irritable and angry, and then something just clicked for you and you realized that what seemed to be caused by other people or things actually had much more to do with your own thoughts and feelings? Perhaps in that brief moment, you were able to change your feelings and in that split second the whole world outside you also seemed to change.

It isn't always easy to see, but when we look at other people in our life, we are actually looking through many lenses, each one tinted by our experiences and each one changing what we see.

We are all very good at projecting unfinished business from our past relationships—with parents, siblings, previous mates, and others—onto our present relationships.

It is okay to be irritable or angry. Having these feelings is part of being human and it is important to honor that part and not deny our humanness. But when we discover how, at times, we project and dump self-anger onto others, we then can begin to take responsibility for our thoughts and projections. Rather than futilely trying to change the other person, we can then begin to change our own self-condemning thoughts. The result is peace of mind.

We can begin to accept the truth that all minds are joined and that the attack thoughts we direct at other people are actually our own attacks on ourselves.

Example

My (Diane's) story about my mom is a perfect example. My mom and I are extremely close, and one day she was telling me how much she loved me and what a wonderful gift I was in her life.

I shared with her that I thought I was probably a gift for her because it was so easy for us to get along but that perhaps her greatest gift was her older sister, Rose, who has been a thorn in her side most of her life. My mom comes from a family of sixteen children. Aunt Rose was up near the top, one of the first children, and my mom was somewhere near the bottom. I asked Mom a question that I often ask myself when I am having difficulties in my own relationships. I said, "Mom, what is it that you dislike the most about Aunt Rose?" I listened intently as she described what she felt those qualities were.

Then I asked Mom what she most feared or disliked about herself. She thought about this for a moment, and then, quite amazed by her own response, she said that the thing she disliked the most in her sister was the very same thing that she most feared and disliked in herself!

Not too long after this experience, my mom and Aunt Rose began to correspond. This opened up a long exchange of letters between them, then phone calls, and finally on a trip back East, my mom visited with her sister, whom she had not seen in twenty-two years.

Recently my mom, in all innocence, said to Jerry and me, "You know, it's a fascinating thing. Of all my brothers and sisters, Rose is the one I have become very close to. I have discovered that we are more alike than any others in the family. In reality, Rose has been one of my best teachers and has helped me see a mirror of myself."

After saying that, she shared the realization that, yes, we do project our lack of tolerance for our own behavior into our relationships. Our own dislike of certain kinds of behavior in ourselves always comes back to us, projected onto others who behave in similar ways.

In this story of Mom and Aunt Rose, we see that other people really do bring us gifts in the form of reflecting our own perceptions back to us. When we choose to receive these gifts, we suddenly have the opportunity to see our own perceptions more clearly. We are able to begin to find ways to forgive ourselves and heal our hurts, and these ways of forgiveness lead us to have peace of mind in our relationships with ourselves as well as others.

Today I will view all my perceptions of other people as if they were mirrored reflections of the thoughts and feelings in my own mind. I will see other people in the present rather than seeing them as shadows of their own pasts or mine.

I CAN CHOOSE TO SEE EVERYONE AS EITHER LOVING OR FEARFUL

Hold no one prisoner.
Release instead of bind,
for thus are you made free.

Our ego is always like a little warrior, suspicious and looking for a good battle, always on the alert, ready to attack and defend. When another person is angry with us, it would have us hold onto the perception that he or she is attacking us and this is an absolute truth that cannot possibly be perceived in any other way. It would convince us that the only logical thing we can do is attack back.

But it is amazing what happens when, for just a moment, we remind ourselves that we can stop listening to the voice of the ego. We can change our perception by choosing to perceive the other person as fearful and giving us a call of help for love. When we do this, we can sense our heart opening up to the warmth of compassion rather than the coldness of anger. The reason for this is simple: We can be helpful and loving to a fearful person, but our humanness will not allow us to feel these things for a person we perceive as attacking us.

When we perceive a person as being fearful whom we formerly perceived as being attacking, a light goes on inside us and we find ourselves seeking ways to be helpful. We discover that we really do have a choice between seeing the world as an attacking-and-defending place or as a place where love and fear exist.

Example

John was notified by the company that had employed him for the past twenty years that some administrative changes were being made and his job was being cut. He would have to seek new employment.

On top of this, John had just learned that his young son had cancer and probably had no more than a few months to live. His company knew this and John was understandably furious. He couldn't believe that the people he'd worked for for all these years could be so unloving during his greatest time of need. John had many people around him to substantiate how awful and unfeeling his company had been.

Suddenly, at the age of 48, he found himself on the job market. When he went for a job interview, he often talked to men and women much younger than himself, and he always felt that they were judging him in a negative way. He believed that they must think that an unemployed man his age could not be very competent.

John called me (Jerry) one night and described the situation he was in. He was being eaten alive with his own anger and resentment. Although he had been a religious man, he began to have grave doubts about the existence of a loving God.

I asked John when he was scheduled for another job interview. He told me that he had one scheduled for the next day. I suggested the following: "When you go in for an interview, don't let getting a job be your first goal."

Surprised, he asked, "What do you mean?"

I replied, "For a moment, stop and consider the possibility that the person interviewing you is fearful. He (or she) may be wondering what would happen to him if he hired you and it doesn't work out, and then he might get fired. So rather than going in there to 'get' something, why don't you see the interviewer as a person who is fearful, giving you a call of help for love. Go to the interview with the idea of *giving* rather than *getting*."

Rather than seeing someone as attacking . . . I can see them as fearful and giving me a call of help for love

John had serious doubts about all this, but he went through with it anyway. The next day he called back with great news: "Your idea worked! I don't know if I got the job, but I was able to see the interviewer as fearful, and I felt a lot of love for him in my heart. I actually enjoyed our time together, and I came away with a tremendous feeling of peace."

Six weeks later he called again with wonderful news. "I got the job and it pays fifteen thousand dollars more than I was earning at my last job."

After John's telephone call, I thought to myself how interesting it is that so many changes occurred in his life the moment he stopped listening to his ego—and started seeing other people not as attacking but as giving a call of help for love. John didn't have to change other people; he only had to change the thoughts in his own mind.

Rather than seeing others as attacking me, I will choose to see them as fearful, giving me a call of help for love.

I CHOOSE TO HAVE PEACE OF MIND AS MY ONLY GOAL

Peace is inevitable
for those who offer peace.

Many of us are in distress because we have multiple goals in our lives. These goals often conflict with one another, and we may feel that no matter what we might do, our actions will just cause us more distress.

Our conflicting goals can also cause us to believe that the source of our distress lies outside our own minds. The result is that no matter which goal we choose, we are going to end up feeling like a victim of people or events in the external world and that the peace of mind we are seeking is completely beyond our control. But the truth is that we can free ourselves from the victim role by choosing to have peace of mind as the only goal in all our relationships. That single goal is the most potent motivating force we can have in our lives.

When we stop to look very closely at ourselves, we often see how goals that seem to make perfect sense to us really are in conflict. Too often the goals we have for creating peace of mind depend on changing the other person. For example, we may want our spouse or friend to be thinner, or more punctual, or to spend less money, or to be more ambitious, or even to pay more attention to us. There are millions of different ways we may want to change our partners, relatives, friends, and business associates. We know only too well how it feels when they fail to respond exactly as we want them to, and they don't live up to a goal we have for them. We get angry, upset, and lose our peace of mind. We may turn around and blame our friend or spouse or business associate for the lack of peace we are experiencing.

When we have one goal of loving someone exactly as he or she is but another goal of wanting to change that person, we can only be in conflict. We are sending the message: "I will love you if you change so that you are behaving in ways that meet my needs." That, of course, is just the opposite of unconditional love. We are telling the other person that we can't love him (or her) as he is; rather, we can give our love only on the condition that he changes.

When the goal is to change another person, we actually give that person the power to determine whether we will be peaceful or not. Our peacefulness will depend on other people changing, or on their behaving in the particular ways that we want them to. We make our experience dependent on whether or not they live up to the conditions we've placed on them. If they do not change to fit our molds, we feel frustrated and angry and once again our peace of mind is nowhere to be found.

If there is a problem in our relationships, our egos come rushing in and tell us that the way to stop our distress is to control, manipulate, and persuade the other person to change to our way of thinking, or to accept our judgments about the way to behave. We feel that the only way to find peace of mind within ourselves is to have the other person completely fulfill our expectations.

When we start feeling that our own peace of mind is dependent on another person changing, it is most helpful to ask ourselves: "What do I need to do right now to find peace of mind and happiness with this person?" This time, the emphasis is on what we can change within ourselves, not on what we think the other person has to change.

To make that choice we only have to let go of our attachment to having the other person change. We have only to remember that peace of mind is our own internal process and need not have anything to do with what is happening outside us. No matter what the circumstances in the external environment, we can always train our minds to choose peaceful thoughts.

When we choose to have peace of mind as our only goal, we are choosing to trust our own power to have that peace within ourselves. We are no longer making our happiness a condition of another person's behavior. We don't have to offer up our anger or frustration "buttons" for other people to push.

The more we are able to love other people for who they really are rather than asking them to change in order to become who we think they should be, the more we will see that we alone are responsible for the thoughts and feelings we experience in our relationships. We create our own anger, depression, and confusion through having conflicting goals.

Peace comes when we stop thinking that it is our goal and obligation to change other people, and when we choose to have peace of mind as our only goal. It is only our own thoughts that we need to change to experience peace.

Example

We have a friend, whom we will call Carol, who lives in New York. She was divorced some years ago and lived with her daughter, Sara. Carol still had tremendous bitterness toward her ex-husband. They rarely spoke, and when they did, they continued to argue about visitation rights and almost everything else. Even though they had been divorced for two years at the time this story took place, they were still trying to change each other. They had anything but peace of mind in their relationship.

Sara, their daughter, participated in our project Children as Teachers of Peace. The final ceremonies of that project were going to take place at the United Nations. Carol was very proud of how involved her daughter had become with wanting to make a difference by doing her part to bring peace to the world.

As preparations for the final ceremonies approached, Carol began to look at the role she was playing in keeping the conflict with her ex-husband alive. If her young daughter Sara could do something about world peace, she reasoned, maybe it was time for Carol to do something about bringing peace to her relationship with Sara's father.

Carol made the choice to call her ex-husband and invite him to the United Nations so that he could see Sara go through the final ceremonies. She did not know how her ex-husband would respond, whether he would yell at her or hang up on her or what. She only knew that peace of mind was going to be her only goal and that she would not react to what he said nor try to change him in any way. She would simply invite him to the ceremonies and would have no attachment to whether he chose to come or not or whether he was happy or got angry at her calling him.

Much to her surprise, her ex-husband did not yell at her, but rather began to cry and then very softly thanked her for the invitation and told her that he would be delighted to go. In fact, he said that he would like to sit with them in the audience at the United Nations.

When Sara awakened the next morning, Carol told her that her father was going to come to see her at the closing ceremonies. Sara replied, "Oh, that's wonderful, but it's too bad you won't be there." She couldn't imagine both her parents in the same room, since they always acted as if they hated each other. So she just assumed that if her father was going to be there, it meant her mother wouldn't be.

"But I will be there," Carol said. "Your father and I are going to be there together."

When Sara heard this, it was almost too much for her to believe. Her parents had never done anything together since their divorce.

That day, at the United Nations, we saw Carol and her ex-husband sitting together, with tears in their eyes as they watched Sara in the ceremonies. They sat side by side, holding hands, peaceful and happy as they enjoyed this moment of union.

Carol demonstrated for herself and everyone else that day that we really can choose to have peace of mind as our only goal. It really is possible to give up goals of changing and blaming, or making our inner peace dependent on other people's actions.

I choose to let go of every goal where my peace of mind depends on other people changing.

I WILL FIND NO VALUE IN BLAMING OTHERS OR MYSELF

As long as you feel guilty,
you are listening to the voice of the ego.

Try to imagine how it would be to live in a world where there was no such thing as blame. How would it be if no one ever looked for ways to blame you for their grievances? And can you imagine being completely free of blaming others for your grievances?

Such a peaceful world is actually possible. We can begin creating it for ourselves when we start recognizing that we don't have to obey our ego when it tells us, "Your purpose in life is to protect yourself by judging who is guilty and who is innocent. Whenever things go wrong for you, the important thing is to be a fault finder. It is important to find someone to blame."

Instead of choosing to listen to the ego, we can remind ourselves that our purpose in life is to forgive and to love. We begin to experience peace and love when we no longer value blame and guilt, knowing that these cannot coexist with love and peace.

Example

A few years ago, I (Jerry) was asked to lead an all-day symposium on Attitudinal Healing in Los Angeles. I drove to the airport early in the morning, left my car there at the parking lot, and returned late that night. When I tried to start my car, I discovered that the battery was dead. I had left the headlights on all day!

Well, I vividly remember what I experienced, and I can tell you that it was anything but peaceful. I was tired after the long day in Los Angeles, and somewhere inside me I thought that I could not have peace of mind until I got my car started and was home in bed.

My ego came rushing in with lightning speed, and I found myself looking for someone to blame. But I was all alone. I remember thinking that if someone had only gone with me to the airport that morning, I could have found all sorts of reasons to blame that person—for talking to me and distracting me so that I had forgotten to turn off my headlights. But I had been all alone that morning, so I had to face the fact that I had no one to blame but myself.

Even though I couldn't find anyone else to blame, I continued to oblige my ego by blaming myself for doing such a stupid thing. I also decided to blame my car, and as I got out to go in search of help, I kicked the front tire, succeeding only in bruising my toe. I quickly realized how dumb that was and turned back to castigating myself.

After I called road service, I calmed down enough to look more carefully at my behavior. I was certainly being attached to guilt and blame, looking for anyone or anything that was the cause of my upset. And I was being anything but loving toward myself.

I finally decided that I really wanted to be peaceful, and I began to realize that I was the only one who could make that happen. I then decided to let go of my old pattern of blaming others or myself when things went wrong. Leaving the headlights on had been a mistake and I could learn from it, but it was not something to feel guilty about.

In the past, I probably would have been angry at myself for days. But this time I was able to forgive myself and let go of my anger right on the spot. In the past, I would have become my own worst enemy and would have forgotten that I cannot have positive, creative relationships with others until I have learned to make friends with myself.

And by the way, I have not left the headlights on in my car again. I suspect that if I hadn't caught myself in my old game of guilt and blame, I wouldn't have learned anything and I probably would have repeated the same old mistakes, running down my battery again and again.

Today I choose to be happy, knowing that I can free myself from judging and blaming other people or myself.

I AM WILLING TO MAKE JOINING, NOT SEPARATION, THE PURPOSE OF ALL MY RELATIONSHIPS

Healing is the effect of minds that join, as sickness comes from minds that separate.

Imagine how the world could be transformed into a place of love and peace if each one of us would choose joining with others as the single goal in all our communications.

Our ego wants us to choose separation as our goal and would have us concentrate on the differences we notice between ourselves and others, in order to reinforce the false reality of separateness. The ego tends to magnify the feeling of separateness by interpreting the world, those in it, and the Source of all Life as untrustworthy. It sees all relationships as potentially dangerous.

The ego believes that its function is to warn us to be on guard, to be hostile, suspicious, mistrusting, defensive, provocative, and attacking. Above all, the ego wants us to always be ready to protect it (the ego) and prove it right. Often, without being totally conscious that we're doing it, we seek the ego's goals.

Joining really means recognizing ourselves in another person and experiencing a sense of oneness with him or her in which our love for that person is as great as our love for ourselves. Joining is finding with another person a mutual or shared way of looking at the world or anything in it. It means being on the constant lookout for what we have in common with each other, rather than concentrating on our differences. Joining is a feeling that goes beyond description. When we experience it, the feelings we share bring us close to the Source of all Life.

For example, I (Jerry), have a space between my two front teeth. When I see another person who has a similar space, I like to point out our similarities and suggest that maybe we came from the same egg.

Children are wonderful teachers of the principle of joining. While traveling with "Children as Teachers of Peace," we often noted how easy it is for children to make friends with other kids they are visiting in foreign countries. They find out what they have in common very quickly, and tend to ignore the differences. In no time they are playing together, having fun, even though they might not even speak the same language.

Likewise, two men came to our center one night. Each appeared to be the exact opposite of the other in every possible way, including their professions, educational backgrounds, the ways they dressed, their social status, etc. On the surface, they appeared to have absolutely nothing in common—and even less to talk about.

A few minutes into the group meeting, however, it became very obvious to us all that these two men were both quite scared, having come to a new place with strangers for the first time. Also, as the evening progressed, they found that they both had a child facing a life-threatening illness and were both feeling helpless in their inability to prevent their child from getting worse. Before our eyes, these two strangers soon became supportive and loving friends who found deep joining and comfort in their common experiences.

Joining doesn't mean that we have to be in complete agreement with everyone or that they have to agree with us. It would be a very boring world if that were the case. But it does mean the joining of our hearts, a feeling of

oneness that comes with recognizing our spiritual reality, which we all share.

Example

At one of our workshops, a woman who was an associate professor of education at a large university told us the following story that has always had a special place in our hearts. She told us that for two years she had an unhealed relationship with a colleague in her department. She said that no matter how hard she tried, she just did not seem able to get along with this man. He was always abrupt, domineering, negative, and just plain nasty to her. She tried to overlook his behavior. She even tried to be "nice" to him, but nothing seemed to work. She returned his nastiness with her own nastiness, and that didn't work either. Finally they established a cold truce, with each party totally ignoring the other. When they passed each other in the hallway, they both looked the other way. She had never experienced anything like this before, and she came to the conclusion there was just "bad chemistry" between them.

Then one day she made up her mind that there had to be a way of looking at this relationship other than carrying around a big bagful of anger and resentment. She had read *Love Is Letting Go of Fear* and she decided to heal some of her attitudes, to stop blaming, and to stop wishing that her colleague would change.

She set herself the goal of changing only the thoughts in her mind. She knew she did not have to change anything about him to feel peaceful and loving in herself. She made up her mind that no matter what his behavior might be, she would send him only love. She decided to see him not as attacking but as fearful. Her single goal was to join her own heart with his, and she was determined that no matter what his outside disguise might be, she was not going to let it affect her.

There were no verbal exchanges between them, but in her daily meditations she decided to visualize her heart sending what she described as "little love hearts" to him. She then visualized a white light surrounding him. As she did this she said silently to herself: "I forgive you. I forgive myself. I love you. I love myself. I release you, and I release myself." She then visualized her colleague getting smaller and smaller and disappearing into a point of light, a point of love. Although there was no change in his behavior, she began to experience a sense of peace that she never had before, and she began to notice that there were no longer any "sharp edges" to her energy when she was around him.

About a month later, she said that she nearly "dropped her teeth" when he stopped her in the hallway and, with a big, friendly smile on his face, told her how much he liked the beautiful blue sweater she was wearing. To her utter astonishment, it was as if their past history of being cold and defensive with each other completely melted away. A brand-new relationship developed, and they began working cooperatively and with great harmony on projects within their department.

My thoughts change my reality

To her, this change in their relationship was a miracle. It was hard for her to understand how their feelings toward each other had changed. She said that the only thing she did was to change her goal to one of joining rather than separation, and to stop interpreting his behavior. All she did was recognize that it was her thoughts about the other person, not the person himself, that caused her pain. And when she chose to do something about her own thoughts, the relationship became one of joining.

In all my communications today, I will have joining as my underlying focus.

THERE IS NO ENEMY EXCEPT THE CONFLICT WITHIN MY OWN MIND

I can be hurt by
nothing but my thoughts.

The ego wants us to believe that everything that makes us unhappy is outside ourselves. It will battle us all the way. It doesn't want us to know that the world we "see" is determined by the thoughts in our own minds. It wants us to believe that everything outside us is the "cause" and what happens to us is the "effect." It would have us always looking in the outside world for the culprit who has done us wrong or for the person who has caused our unhappiness.

Have you ever noticed that on days when you truly feel at peace within yourself the people and situations that usually bother you no longer cause you distress? If you are a parent, maybe you've noticed how your children's noise can drive you crazy on some days but you hardly notice it at all on the days you are feeling peaceful. The level of noise your kids are making can be exactly the same in both cases. The only difference is your state of mind.

Our state of mind has everything to do with how we react and how we experience the world. When we are at peace with ourselves, things that happen to us do not seem to have such a sharp edge to them. We find that instead of putting energy into negativity, we are putting our energy into maintaining inner peace.

Like most people, you have probably had the experience

of going to bed at night feeling conflict rather than peace. Maybe you were feeling guilty because you were late for work or for an appointment. You may have had an argument with someone and later realized that you had made a mistake. Or maybe you went to bed with feelings of murderous rage and revenge because you believed that someone had done something to hurt you.

Perhaps you wake up the next morning feeling angry and upset but immediately deny those feelings to yourself. Then the first person you meet that day says, "My, but you are irritable this morning! What happened to you? Did you get up on the wrong side of the bed?" And you reply: "No, I'm just fine! You're the one who is irritable."

Later in the day you feel more at peace within yourself and you awaken to the truth that, indeed, you are the one who was irritable all along. Your ego just projected the feelings that resulted from the battles within your own mind out onto the other person.

When we have inner peace, there are no battles between conflicting thoughts going on in our minds. But when those inner battles are going strong, our ego does its very best to project those conflicts onto people and situations. We then do our level best to find fault in someone else and feel justified in our anger. When we find these situations, it is easy to believe the ego and deny that the cause of what we are experiencing is within our own minds.

Example

After a workshop on healing relationships that we presented at the University of California in Santa Barbara, a man named Michael, who was about forty years of age, took us to the airport. On the way, he told us the following story.

In high school, Michael had been a track star and had

won all sorts of ribbons. He was very proud of his track accomplishments, and they were a major source of his self-esteem. But he said that one of the biggest grievances and sorrows in his life had been that his father had never once gone to any of his track meets. He had carried this hurt with him for years.

One year, he went back to his hometown to attend his twentieth high school reunion and was surprised to find that his old coach was there. His coach asked him how his father was doing. Michael acted surprised and said to his coach, "I didn't even know that you knew my father!"

His coach stared back at him in disbelief, then replied, "Well, of course I knew him! He attended every track meet you were ever in."

Michael said, "Coach, I'm sorry, but you must be confused. You've got him mixed up with someone else's father. You see, my dad never came to a single track meet of mine, and this has been a real sore spot with me for many years."

The coach stood his ground. "Michael," he said, "I'm not the one who is confused. Your dad (and he called him by his first name) was one of our most loyal fans!"

Michael went to his father's house that night and told his dad about the conversation he had had with his coach.

With tears in his eyes, Michael's dad said, "Your coach is right, Michael. You see, I did go to every single one of your track meets. I was so very proud of you. But I always stood behind the bleachers because I didn't want to embarrass you."

In his youth, Michael's father had come to the United States from another country. He had always felt shy and insecure because he spoke English with a thick accent and had never quite gotten over the feeling of being a "foreigner." Until that moment, Michael had never realized how self-conscious his father had felt about this.

Michael went on to tell us that for years he had made his

father his enemy, based on his own perceptions of why he had never seen his father at track meets. He said that since the workshop he realized that the enemy was not his dad but the negative thoughts in his own mind.

Michael's story reminds us that our perceptions never see anything as a whole, and what we see is determined by what we believe. Many people go for years with unhealed relations because of mistaken perceptions like Michael's.

Today I will remind myself that the anger I may feel is caused by a battle within my own mind. I can choose not to project it onto other people.

TODAY I CHOOSE TO TEAR UP MY SCRIPTS FOR OTHER PEOPLE

My forgiveness is the means
by which the world is healed,
together with myself. Let me,
then, forgive the world,
that it may be healed along with me.

One of the most common difficulties in relationships comes from the ego's belief that it knows best what other people should do, how they should act and think, and even how their bodies should look. The arrogant ego would have us believe that only our own scripts should be followed, that they are the best ones and everyone else should keep in step with our music.

Sometimes we are so convinced that our own scripts are the only right ones that we will reject, criticize, attack, or make an enemy of anyone who fails to conform to our wishes. This is usually difficult for us to detect in ourselves because the ego is so good at hiding the truth from our awareness.

Frequently, when others don't follow our scripts we begin to dehumanize them, treating them as objects. Before long, there is a complete absence of emotion in our relationship, and we end up communicating with each other only with our head rather than our heart.

Example

My (Jerry's) mother lived to be ninety-seven years of age, and she continues to be one of the most important teachers in my life. During the last years of her life, she lived in a retirement home, and there was a time when she managed to make everyone who visited her feel guilty. Regardless of how much time they spent with her, it was never enough. After a while, most of her friends and relatives stopped visiting her.

When we went to visit her, we frequently ended our visits feeling worn out from her complaints and lack of satisfaction, regardless of how peaceful we felt when we arrived. There was a part of us that wanted her to be a peaceful little old lady, and my mom was determined that that was not going to be her script.

One day as we were meditating, just before visiting my mom, it became clear to both Diane and me that we were trying to please mom at the same time that we were trying to change her. That was not unconditional love. We had been trying to write a script for my mother. Our script was that we wanted her to be happy during her last years and we wanted very much to please her. We reminded ourselves that unconditional love meant accepting people exactly as they are. Where my mom was concerned, this meant accepting her decision to suffer.

Diane and I decided to tear up our scripts for my mom and we chose, instead, to have inner peace as our only goal in our relationship with her. Our peace of mind no longer depended on my mother's behavior. As a matter of fact, her behavior didn't change at all. After our visits with her we began to feel peaceful and full of energy.

Soon after we stopped trying to write my mom's scripts, an amazing thing began to happen. She asked for my tapes and books. This was a new thing for her. Prior to this she had refused to have much to do with them at all. She even asked for extra copies of the books and tapes so that other people in the retirement home could enjoy them. In the process, she also healed her relationship with the head nurse. Her complaints began to disappear and she began to be loving, tender, and grateful during our visits.

Today I choose to tear up my scripts for other people and accept them as they are

Isn't it fascinating that when we stop trying to change other people, our relationships become much more loving and open, and healthy change that we could never have predicted comes about?

Today I will let go of my desire to have other people follow my scripts for them. I will do my best to remember that when I accept others as they are, I allow myself and those around me to experience unconditional love.

TODAY I FORGIVE MY PARENTS TOTALLY, RELEASING US ALL FROM THE PAST

❦

Forgiveness is the means by which
I will recognize my innocence.

Many of us have had childhood experiences that made us wish that our parents could have been more loving toward us. And some of us carry the scars of traumatic events that continue to rage inside us with the fire of resentment. These events may seem so unforgivable that the ego tries to convince us that we must hold on forever to our resentments and pain.

When the fearful child is kept alive within us even in adulthood, it becomes very difficult to have totally loving relationships. The pain from our childhood becomes a barbed wire fence, preventing anyone from coming anywhere near our hearts. Beyond this fence, currents of mistrust roam the caverns of our minds, making it difficult for us to open our hearts to others. Our ego's voice is often there, crying out its warning to remember our unforgivingness and hold onto it so that we can never be hurt again.

Many people have had horrendous experiences, such as incest, physical and emotional abuse, abandonment and rejection. Certainly it is easy to label such acts as unforgivable, and to keep the pain they caused within us forever. The ego would falsely have us believe that if we were ever to forgive such horrendous acts we would actually be condoning them, perhaps even allowing them to happen again.

Sometimes painful childhood experiences are locked in the vaults of our mind, where the original pain roars just as loudly as ever but is somehow hidden from our conscious thoughts. The fearful child that may live within every one of us needs our nurturing and our care, whether we hear its voice clearly or not. As part of this nurturing we can choose to unlock the vaults within our mind and process the emotions and pain that we are hiding there.

By this we mean that it is important to honor our human emotions of anger, terror, and helplessness. We cannot free ourselves of these painful experiences by repressing them or by dumping the anger we feel on others.

Sometimes having imaginary conversations with the people who originally hurt us can be helpful. At other times we may find it helpful to write down what we feel and tear up the paper or burn it, acknowledging our pain to ourselves but also letting it go. At other times some form of counseling can help. To heal our past hurts, it is not necessary for the person who has hurt us to be involved at all. It is only our own perceptions and our own fearful inner child that needs to be cared for and healed.

It is important to decide what we want to do with our feelings of fear, anger, and helplessness from our past. Do we really want to put these feelings back into our mental vaults so that they can continue singing their angry songs and dancing their angry dances? Or do we want to ask for help from that wise Inner Teacher that each of us carries in our hearts? When we are at last willing to forgive and hand over our pain to a Higher Power, we pass through the dark cloud and find the light once again.

We know a woman whose father attempted to seduce her when she was thirteen years old. Her father warned her never to tell her mother, but the girl did so anyway. Shortly thereafter, the father left home and her parents were divorced. The little girl blamed herself for the divorce, believing that it was because she had told her mother what her father had done that this happened. For such a long time, she was unable to resolve the pain of that experience and the guilt she felt for "causing" her parents' breakup.

She was more than thirty years old when she went to her mother to discuss what had happened and how it had affected her life. Her mother told her that when her father was thirteen years old, he was sexually molested by an older woman. All of a sudden this woman who had been sexually violated by her father no longer saw her dad as a "sexual pervert," which up until then had been her view of him. Now she saw him as a very frightened and confused child living in the body of an adult.

With her new understanding, she was able to do something that she had never dreamed she could ever do. She opened the vaults within her mind and forgave her father. This does not mean that she condoned what he did: on the contrary. But she was able to let go of the anger and pain she felt and at last be free of it. She had not seen her father for many years, but she sought him out, wrote to him, and later went to visit him. When she saw him, she no longer saw a horrible human being but found instead a frightened child within her father. The relationship became healed and now they visit each other regularly.

We believe that we all really do the very best job that we know how to do. Many people find it much easier to forgive when they see the real meaning of this statement, that if we had the same childhood experiences, with the same parenting that our parents received, we might very well have made the same mistakes that we find so difficult to forgive.

Example

It is not necessary for both people to participate in healing an unhealed relationship. Healing can take place when the

other person is on the opposite side of the world or even if
they have died. I (Diane) had a firsthand experience with
this in my own life. I'd like to relate that story to you.

My father died when I was nineteen years old. He and I
had an unhealed relationship, and it wasn't until many
years after his death that I realized how unhealed it really
had been. When I first realized this, I felt despondent,
believing that since my dad had died it was impossible for
me to do anything about it.

Looking back on my childhood, I realized that I had a
strange sort of silence about my feelings toward my dad. I
felt that I'd come to terms with his death. I felt that I had let
him go, but I still felt something missing inside me. It was
as if a part of my heart was locked up. And it was clear to
me that the key for unlocking it was in my dad's and my
unhealed relationship. So how could I get that key and
unlock my heart when it involved someone who was not
here anymore?

I gave a lot of time to remembering my childhood. When I
was small, there was a lot of physical violence in our family.
Interactions between different family members were often
anything but peaceful. Because I was the youngest child, I
didn't directly receive my father's wrath, but I lived in fear
of my father's personality erupting like a volcano.

Inside me there had grown a tremendous amount of anger and resentment, but it was very quiet, very well hidden,
because there had never been a safe place where I could
express it. As I grew older, I realized that this was locking
up the unconditional love within my heart, stopping the
flow of love for everyone in my life. I tried every possible
way I could find to release it.

As with many children who grow up in this kind of
environment, I went into my mind, my intellect, running
away from those painful places in my heart. In my intellect,
I was sure I understood everything that had occurred in my

childhood. I could have gotten a Ph.D. in family dynamics. But even with all the facts, I still didn't feel good. It's that feeling when you know something in your head but just can't feel it in your heart.

I remember an occasion when Jerry was thinking about writing his book *Goodbye to Guilt* and he was asking everyone around him, "What in your life do you still feel guilty about?" When he asked me, I was shocked at my reply. I said that I felt most guilty about wanting my dad to be someone other than who he was. I wanted him to be like my friend Christine's father, who lived across the street and was very peaceful and calm.

A short time afterward, just before I went to sleep one night, I made a statement out loud that I clearly knew that I alone could not heal my relationship with my dad. I had done everything mentally possible, but something was missing. It was as though I had the 1, 2, 3, and 5, but the number 4 was missing and it wasn't anywhere in the world to be found.

I remember opening my hands, raising them in the air, and saying to the Creator, "I can't do this alone. I'm asking for your help. I know that your plan for me is perfect happiness. I know that you want me to be happy and whole so that I can receive your love and give your love to others. You've probably told me how to do all this many times in the past and perhaps I wasn't listening, but I am listening now, and whatever you tell me I will do. I will listen this time." I went to sleep with that thought.

That night I woke up sobbing. When you grow up as I did, you don't cry a lot. It simply wasn't a part of my behavior. So it was very unusual for me to wake up in tears. I thought I was literally drowning in a river of tears, and what kept running through my mind was: "Dad, if I could just walk with you one more time!"

These thoughts just wouldn't go away. I continued to

cry, and at last I got up and began to write, the words just flowing out as I sat there sobbing. When I was done writing, I looked at what I'd written and realized that it was a prayer of forgiveness, a total letting go and a total joining.

How many of us have had the feelings that we wanted either our mother or our father or both of them to be different? That had been my pain. I had wanted my dad to be different, to be other than who he was. Somehow, in my writing, I found it in my heart to let go of that, and to let my dad be completely himself. My forgiveness was for my thoughts and my judgments that I had placed on him, and my forgiveness was for myself. Dad didn't have to change at all in order for me to be happy.

I would like to share my poem about my dad and I with you who might still have an unhealed relationship with either of your parents. It is a little like the Father's Day card that Hallmark will never write. It is called "If I Could Walk With You, Dad."

> If I could walk with you, Dad,
> A moment from time stolen free,
> I'd feel the pace you walked,
> And I'd find it soothing for me.
>
> At the edge of day,
> In the low August sun,
> Weary from work,
> And your chores to be done,
>
> Your pleasures were small
> And they seemed so worthless to me,
> Yet, as I reach each day,
> It is they that set me free.

Your flowers, their gardens,
From baked clay you gave them life;
Your birds, their wings,
God's instruments in flight.

We spoke so little,
And we shared even less.
If I could walk with you, Dad,
My heart would confess,

That I never understood your anger
Or your frustrations or your pain.
But as confusing as it was,
I only have gained.

Because you forced me to go inward,
To search and to find
The meaning of life,
Of love, and of time.

You taught me without teaching
And you gave me from inside
Many meanings to this journey
Though you never knew why.

You were my gardener,
And my tender, and my teacher, untold,
From your heart and your hands,
My spirit you helped mold.

In my fragile cocoon,
Protected from strife,
I heard from inside
The meaning of life.

So I give to you now,
As we walk tonight, Dad,
My heart, our connection,
Never again sad.

The past is gone,
And I've laid it to rest
'Cause we both know now
We did our beautiful best.

And I stand on the crest
Of the hills of my mind,
And I wave you on
In your journey in time,

To find your family
In light, all around,
In love and peace and forgiveness,
May you always abound.

When I read the poem the next morning—interestingly enough, it was written on the night that would have been my dad's seventieth birthday—I felt an incredible release. It was very clear to me that everything that had happened between me and my dad had been absolutely perfect just as it was. The poem was my final acceptance that everything we experienced together had been an opportunity for me to learn, to grow, if I chose to see it that way. When I finally was able to take responsibility for cocreating our relationship, I realized I wasn't a victim of the world, and I wasn't a victim of the relationship. I realized that there was no way that I could now do the work I do in healing relationships if I had not experienced this relationship with my dad. So I am forever grateful for the experience we had together.

There is one final thing I'd like to share with you about

that relationship. Having gone across the bridge of forgiveness, I can now feel my dad's presence with me in all the work I do. I feel his love guiding me, knowing that he was one of my greatest teachers. It is within this context that I say to others that it is possible for one person to completely heal a relationship.

The love we give is always received, on some level of consciousness, and it is only our ego that tells us that the other person needs to respond in some particular way or else the relationship cannot be healed. It only takes one, and you have the power within you to heal any relationship in your life. Healing a relationship is a singular choice, and each one of us really can choose once again.

Today I send love and forgiveness to my parents, whether they are living or not. I will remember that forgiveness releases us all from the past.

TODAY I WILL CHOOSE NOT TO BE KING OR QUEEN OF THE PROCRASTINATORS' CLUB

Doubt is the result of conflicting wishes. Be sure of what you want, and doubt becomes impossible.

When we really believe that this instant is the only time that there is, it becomes much clearer to us how important it is to choose to be happy now, not later. Our ego, however, is always urging us to hold onto the past or to fear the future. It is always telling us, "Well, you really can wait until tomorrow to decide to do that." Or, "I want you to remember that this person really hurt you, and he will just do it again if you forgive him. He deserves your anger. And if you are really going to insist on forgiving him, wait a little while. Wait at least until tomorrow."

The decision to procrastinate about forgiving is a decision to be unhappy. Whenever we procrastinate we are making a decision to suffer. Holding onto unforgiving thoughts and grievances is a decision to continue to be in conflict. It is choosing fear instead of love, unhappiness instead of happiness.

Many years ago, I (Jerry) was the ship's surgeon for the Matson Navigation Line. The ship I was on, the *Matsonia*, had been nicknamed by the crew "the ship for newlyweds and nearly deads." As the ship's surgeon, I saw many elderly people who had sacrificed most of their youth, waiting for their retirement years when they could travel and enjoy themselves. Their attitude toward life was to wait

We will continue to be unhappy until we choose to forgive

until later to enjoy themselves and be happy. The problem was that with most of these couples, one or the other of them was ill or physically limited and not able to fully enjoy this relaxed time they had put off for the last portion of their lives.

The time to be happy and joyful is always now. It is not something that can be put off until later. Forgiveness is the key to our happiness, and it is an important part of our decision to be joyful in our lives each day. We will continue to be unhappy until we no longer put off the decision to completely forgive those we feel have hurt us.

Example

We had a friend named Rafael Soriano, a famous architect whom we greatly admired. He recently died, in his seventies. His was the heart of a child, which he kept youthful and alive every moment of the day. He lived each second of each day, putting 100 percent of himself into being happy and loving to all he encountered. A kind and gentle man, he believed that one of his missions in life was to put a smile on the face of everyone he met.

He dearly loved his garden and would hand a beautiful flower to every man, woman, and child who passed by, as if every single one of them was the most important, beautiful, and lovely person in the world. Rafael made everyone feel simply wonderful and totally loved. He was always smiling and singing.

He was determined not to let life pass him by. As far as we could see, he actively chose to be totally happy, full of humor and a zest for life every second of every day. Rafael understood the power of forgiveness and the power of love as well as anyone we have ever known. It was as though he had made the decision never to procrastinate about life, choosing instead to let go of all grievances.

He was a wonderful teacher to all who were privileged to know him.

Today I make the decision to be happy, choosing to forgive and to love instead of being the king or queen of the procrastinators' club.

12

HELPING OTHERS IS THE WAY I HEAL MYSELF

Your interpretations of our brother's needs are your interpretations of yours. By giving help you are asking for it.

The belief system of love is based on the premise that in all our relationships we can have the same interest in others' lives as we have in our own. We both believe, with all our hearts, that the peak experiences in life, where we feel the highest forms of pure joy, love, and inner peace, come when we are reaching out and helping another person. It is in this experience that we experience our own greatest healings.

Let us remember that *healing*, in this book, refers to the mind, not the body. Peace of mind, our most profound experience of this healing, occurs the moment that we focus on helping others, rather than on becoming preoccupied with our own problems.

As we learn to concentrate on solutions, rather than on our own problems, we discover that our giving of love is always the answer to any of our problems, regardless of their form. Holding out your hand to help another is a very direct way of finding peace of mind for yourself and dissolving any negative thoughts.

To create the experiences of helping others it is most helpful to have in the forefront of your mind at all times the goal of being helpful to whomever you are with at the present moment. It means having in your consciousness, with every breath you take, the question, "How can I be of service to others?"

The belief system of the heart is based on unconditional love, with a perception of ourselves as global citizens, each with a passionate desire to be helpful and loving toward everyone, no matter where they might live in the world.

As we write this, there are close to sixty independent Centers for Attitudinal Healing around the world, all staffed primarily by volunteers. In these centers we have seen people in severe physical pain from cancer, in deep emotional pain from divorce or the death of loved ones, and in deep depression from lack of money or a job. Yet we have seen them be totally uplifted when they put all their energy into helping others and being of service to them.

When we make the decision to live one second at a time, and in that instant to be concerned only with extending our love to others and being of service to them, a marvelous thing occurs. We discover that we are no longer absorbed in our own body and our own problems.

This is in sharp contrast to the ego's belief system, which tells us to think of ourselves and our nuclear families first, and then maybe consider helping others—if they are worthy of our help. The ego tries to convince us that we are just too busy to take the time to be helpful to others. The ego believes in a "me first" world. The idea that "as we give, so we receive" is completely foreign to it.

When we are totally absorbed in helping others, we find that we can experience peace and joy that sometimes seems beyond our wildest imaginings.

Example

A short time ago, I (Diane) was in Palo Alto, California, on business. I had planned one of those impossible days, where there was no way I could accomplish everything I had set out to do.

I was rushing to an appointment, my mind going a hundred miles an hour, when I noticed a very frail, elderly man leaning against a building. He held tightly to his walker and looked as if the wind could blow him off his feet any minute. In a less rushed, more normal state of mind, I would have stopped and offered to help him. As I passed him that day, however, I remember thinking, "Oh, my God, I hope he doesn't ask for my help. I'm too busy to stop today." I went by and all of a sudden I heard him call out: "Could you please help me?"

I stopped, reminding myself that everything is perfect just the way it is, knowing that we create exactly the world we need. I stopped, turned, and asked him: "How can I help you?" He looked at me and, apparently sensing the hurry I was in, said, "Oh, no, I don't want to bother you." Part of my split mind said, "Oh, good, here is your opportunity to turn around and go the other way. Go ahead, take it!"

I said to the man, "No, that's okay. You are not bothering me at all. I have time for you. How can I help?"

"Well," he said, "I am trying to get across the street to that building." He pointed to indicate the place where he wanted to go. "That's where I live." It was a wide and busy intersection.

I replied, "Well, I would be glad to go there with you." We could not have gone more slowly. It took twenty-one minutes to cross the intersection.

As we crossed the street, I began smiling, and I thought, "What a beautiful teacher of love and healing this person is for me, teaching me not to be in quite such a hurry with my life." I suddenly felt grateful for this time to be with him, and as I left him I felt so peaceful and loving, healed from the split mind I had created with my impossible

**When you help and give your heart to others, the desire to
complain and blame simply disappears**

schedule. I mentally noted that it is the schedule I create for myself that often serves to sabotage my own peace of mind.

Until I met this man, I was totally preoccupied with all the things I had to do, running down the street as if the only thing in the world was me and my business. This man and his simple need gave me the opportunity to change my mind, to come back into the present, to find a moment of love and peace through helping another person.

Today, no matter whom I'm with, I will remind myself of the single question, "How can I be of service to others?"—remembering that in helping others I heal myself.

I CAN BE
FREE OF
SUFFERING
TODAY

All fear is past because its source is gone,
and all its thoughts are gone with it.
Love remains the only present state.

We are never upset for the reasons we think. If we are upset with something that has happened in a relationship, it is because of unfinished business from our own past, and we can be free of suffering by letting go of the past. It is helpful to know that our unforgiving thoughts are at the root of our suffering. Our egos urge us to keep pain and fear alive, believing that this is the only way we can protect ourselves from getting hurt again. Our spiritual self, however, reminds us that suffering disappears the moment we forgive ourselves and others.

Many of us seem to choose people in our love relationships, friendships, and even at work, with whom we unconsciously try to reenact hurtful past conflicts in order to resolve them. The conflict may have nothing to do with the person in front of us.

We heal conflicts in our relationships only by going back to their source. Denying that the real problem is in our past only allows the same conflict to continue, arising again and again in our relationships. We tend to use denial of this kind when we feel that the hurts of the past are so painful that we simply can't look at them. There is a part of us that wants to keep old conflicts buried because we feel so hopeless about being able to heal them.

Example

During a workshop on healing relationships that we held recently in the Midwest, a Catholic nun in her seventies told our group her own story about going inside to complete old, unfinished business. With much shy determination, she spoke of the pain she harbored as a result of the anger and impatience she had toward her older sister, who was also a retired nun. When we asked her if she was willing to explore this further, she said that she had prayed that very morning for help in releasing herself from her pain.

Through role playing we helped her explore her old grievances with her sister. Another person played the role of her sister, and she recaptured some of the feelings that she had been holding inside herself, in the prison of her own mind. We explored further and further back in time until we reached the point where it had all started.

When the nun was around seven years old, her father told her and her sister that he would pay a dime to have his shoes polished well. As the nun told it, she was the one who polished her father's shoes while her sister was the one who got the dime. She also perceived that her sister received her father's love and all the special attention that went with it. Unbeknownst to her, all the anger she had felt toward her sister throughout her whole life went back to the dime and the shoes and everything that story represented to her. As she went back to being that seven-year-old, she was able to shout and get rid of some angry feelings that she had held inside all these years.

For the first time in her life, the woman felt a true willingness to forgive and to let go of the past. During this encounter we witnessed, along with hundreds of others, an angular, rigid woman, who seemed to have so many sharp angles about her, begin to soften. It seemed as if everything in her body suddenly became rounder and she seemed to grow younger right before our eyes.

A younger member of the community told us that this sister had been one of the most difficult people to live with. She always gave an extremely hard time to anyone who seemed "privileged" or who was treated "special" in any way. No one had ever been able to understand why she was so critical when issues of this sort came up. Now everything fell into place.

The nun who told us her story later spoke to her community about her experience and her newly healed relationship with her sister. Shortly after healing the relationship in her own mind, she visited with her sister and they experienced a beautiful joining. It never ceases to amaze us how powerful our willingness to heal old grievances held in our minds can be for healing our relationships in the present.

I can be free of suffering today by letting go of all my unforgiving thoughts.

FORGIVENESS OFFERS ME EVERYTHING I WANT

**To hold a grievance is to
let your ego rule your mind.**

What is it that you want from life? Do you want happiness? Do you want peace of mind? And do you want to experience loving relationships, with an absence of tension and hostility?

Forgiveness offers all this and more to every one of us. It is the key to solving all our problems. It not only offers the key to happiness and joy, but it offers the key to our physical well-being, allowing us to feel balance and harmony between body, mind, and spirit. It is the key to our freedom, allowing us to soar like eagles. It allows us to tear down the barbed wire fences we have built around our hearts.

For just a moment, stop and think about a relationship where you are still experiencing unforgiving thoughts. As you think about this relationship, you may feel that holding on to your grievance gives you what you want. Maybe you feel hurt about the "hand that life has dealt you," or maybe you feel that another person's actions have caused you to suffer.

Maybe you still feel that your suffering is because your parents didn't love you enough. Maybe you have suffered the pain of a divorce or a rejection in your work or personal life. Maybe you suffered pain and even anger because someone very close to you has moved away or because someone you loved has died.

As your grievances bubble to the surface, notice how they make you feel. Our egos do not want us to notice that holding onto our grievances is actually a decision to hold onto pain and to keep peace and happiness away.

The choice to forgive or to hold onto grievances is a conscious one. When we choose to hold onto our grievances, we fill our minds with pain, conflict, and suffering. When we choose to forgive, we immediately feel lighter, as if tons have been lifted from our backs. The moment we forgive, all pain and suffering caused by our grievances disappears.

When we choose forgiveness, we are choosing to stop projecting our inner conflicts onto the outside world, and we are freeing ourselves of the prison of our own thoughts and feelings.

Example

A friend, whom we'll call Will, told us the following story: He and his wife were divorced. Their children, who were four and six years old at the time, lived with their mother. Will's ex-wife was remarried to a man twenty years older than her, who turned out to be an alcoholic. The new husband verbally abused the children, and Will felt extremely angry at his wife for marrying such a man. But he felt helpless about being able to do anything about it.

One day he made a decision to embark on a spiritual path in his life, and he heard a little voice within him reminding him to love his enemies. All of a sudden he got it: If he was going to love and forgive his enemies, this included his ex-wife. He knew this would be a difficult task because she was at the top of the list. Nevertheless, he began the daily practice of thinking about her with a sense of forgiveness.

Every day he visualized her surrounded by a pure white light, which was his image of forgiveness and peace. Gradually, he felt his own resentment and anger toward her disappearing.

About two months after he started this process of forgiveness, he received a friendly telephone call from his ex-wife. She told him that she had left her new husband to start a new life for herself and the children. She asked Will's forgiveness and expressed hope that in the future their conversations would be more friendly and cooperative than they had been in the past.

Will told us that he was absolutely amazed at the power of forgiveness. He told us that in the beginning he did not think he could ever forgive his ex-wife, but then he reminded himself that forgiveness was a choice that he could willingly make.

Today I will have a willingness to totally forgive anyone with whom I am still holding onto a grievance.

I WILL BE STILL FOR AN INSTANT

Only be quiet. You will need no rule
but this, to let your practicing today
lift you above the thinking of the world
and free your vision from the body's eyes.
Only be still and listen.

From the moment we awaken each morning to the time that we go to sleep at night, our minds are filled with thoughts that influence the many decisions that we make during the day. For most of us, these thoughts go in many different directions, and many are in conflict with each other, causing discord. On close inspection, we may also discover that many of our thoughts are based on negative experiences from the past, yet we often let them influence our decisions in the present.

The day-to-day busyness of our lives often makes our thoughts even more scattered. We find our mind wandering and would like to have better control of it. To some of us, however, it seems like an impossible task to control our minds. It almost seems as if there are just too many stimuli to cope with, too many things we want to do, and we run out of breath rushing around to get things accomplished.

To retrain our minds to be still and peaceful, rather than busy and confused, takes desire and self-discipline. A disciplined mind is a free mind, a mind no longer tied in knots. A disciplined mind is free of conflict, allowing its creativity to be nourished in the quietude of love.

We love the often-quoted statements that "A busy mind is a sick mind. A slow mind is a healthy mind. And a still mind is a divine mind."

There are many times when we say we want a quiet, peaceful mind, but we do not really mean it. When we *truly* want a still and peaceful mind, with all of our being, our minds will become still and peaceful. When we are still for an instant, the busy world around us begins to disappear. Then we can find ourselves in a state of perfect stillness—silent and at peace—where there are no words, no doubts, and no fears.

When we are still for an instant we enjoy a state of mind that is a perfect haven from all the busyness of the world to which we have been exposed. It feels like "home" because, in that still instant, we have once again returned to that place of peace and love that always abides in the center of our hearts and is our true home. In retraining our minds, it is so important that we remember, as often as we can, to

Happiness is found when you live in the present

value being still for an instant and to feel the peace that is in the silence.

Example

We would like to suggest that you become your own example. If you are willing, please put this book down and close your eyes for a moment. Have the desire to truly want to be still for an instant and to experience a peaceful mind. Take a few deep breaths and focus on having a willingness to let go of the external world for an instant.

During this instant, allow yourself to feel the quietness of a still lake with a beautiful swan crossing it. Feel the oneness of nature and allow yourself to feel a part of all that is.

In the beauty of this silence, quietly say to yourself, "I will be still for an instant and go home."

Today I will remind myself, as often as I can, to be still for an instant, because I truly want to experience the benefits of a peaceful mind.

EPILOGUE

Deep within you is everything
that is perfect, ready to radiate
through you and out into the world.

As we forgive and let go of our illusions of separation, we can begin to awaken to the reality that all of our relationships exist in order to reflect the love inherent in the Ultimate Relationship, our true relationship with our Source. Here we find that there are no illusions, and none can ever enter.

Let us help each other to let go of all fear and to experience the limitless, eternal love that is our natural inheritance. Let us help each other return to the home of love, deep in our hearts, that we never really left.

Let us awaken from the sleep of forgetfulness and dedicate ourselves to a new willingness to remember God's unending love and forgiveness. Let us help each other resist the temptation to judge others or to withhold our love from anyone.

With every breath, with every heartbeat, and with every step that we take, let us make forgiveness and love the singular message of each day. May the light of our love always shine brightly so that there may be no more darkness anywhere.

Let us see the total innocence of a child and the face of God in everyone we meet or even think about. In all our relationships, let us embrace each other with our love as we celebrate our joining, our oneness, and our joy.

Let the bells of certainty ring loud and clear, filling our hearts as we tell one another and ourselves, "No matter what the question, love is the answer."

Whatever the *question*, love is the answer.
Whatever the *problem*, love is the answer.
Whatever the *illness*, love is the answer.
Whatever the *pain*, love is the answer.
Whatever the *fear*, love is the answer.
Love is always the answer because
Love is all there is.

I am created as love, and love knows no boundaries and never dies

FROM THE
AUTHORS

Writing this book has brought much healing into both of our lives. We wrote it for people who, like ourselves, believe that there has to be a better way of living in this world and who are willing and determined to find that way.

We wrote it for those who are willing to look anew at their beliefs and to perhaps learn to choose only those that will bring peace of mind, love, and happiness into their lives and the lives of those around them.

As we came together to write about relationships, we were once again reminded that we teach what we want to learn. In our own lives, there are still many days when we struggle with the challenge of choosing harmony, acceptance, and love in all our relationships, with both the new people in our lives and with those relationships that go back to our very earliest years. It is rarely easy because, all too often, when something goes wrong, there is still the temptation to find someone to blame, or to judge and condemn ourselves.

Although we had lived and worked in the same small town since 1975, it wasn't until August 20, 1981, that we met. In many respects, we were the most unlikely prospects imaginable for a relationship. We entered the world from two different decades, from opposite sides of the continent, influenced by two different faiths, and torn by two different wars. Yet, we found that we shared many of the same feelings, life goals, joys, and sorrows.

The first two-and-a-half years of our relationship were stormy and filled with conflict. Then things began to change as we discovered that many of our conflicts actually had to do with previous relationships in our lives that we had not yet healed. We began to discover the power of forgiveness, how to change the thoughts in our minds and, as a result, our lives began to change.

In spite of our differences in background, age and life experience, we discovered that we both had lives that, like so many other people we knew, were filled with the pain, hurt, tears, and turmoil that come from unhealed relationships. As we wrote this book we became increasingly aware of how our childhoods, as well as much of our adult lives, have been filled with experiences that caused us to feel fearful of intimate relationships and to be afraid of love.

We were both the youngest of three children, and we deeply felt the scars of families where there was a single domineering force; for Jerry this domineering force was his mother, for Diane it was her father. For each of us, it has taken painful relationships, a failed marriage, and an intense willingness to relate to each other in open and honest ways not previously found in order to begin to experience that there really is another way of relating to each other and the world.

During the many workshops and lectures that we have given together over the years, we have experienced the courage of others as they exposed their deepest inner selves in order to grow. These people inspired us to open our own inner doors, shedding light on the skeletons in our own closets. We came to recognize the many times we had given up an important part of ourselves in order to get what we thought we needed in order to feel safe. The wrenching pain of exposing the control mechanisms we so cleverly created in order to survive emotionally in dysfunctional families became an opportunity to transform our skills into tools for transformation for ourselves and, gradually, for many others in our lives.

The current status of people's parental relationships, whether healed or unhealed, directly reflects on all of their current relationships. As we have traveled around the world lecturing, we have frequently asked our audiences, "How many of you still have unhealed relationships with one or both of your parents?" Regardless of the country or the culture that we are in, no fewer than 75 percent of the people raise their hands.

As we both recognized that there was more healing for us to do in regard to our own parents, we have been able to see the frightened child inside each other. Perhaps one of the most important aspects of our relationship has been learning to become trusted friends. Through much hard work we have begun to experience the freedom that is created through honesty, and the desire to continue our relationship, that has come about by creating safe and open spaces for each other.

An important key to resolving conflicts that come up between us has been a new willingness, on the part of both of us, to ask each other for help. The simple words "I need your help" puts us in an entirely different space when we feel attacked and we want to dump our anger on each other.

We are not always successful, but we do our best to continue to be open, to learn each day how to love and let go, how not to hold on, and how to have a relationship where there are no demands or assumptions. We have as our joint goal the peace of God, and our wills are joined as one to be of service to others.

We have been truly blessed by having so many wonderful

friends and teachers of love who have come into our lives and have joined us in finding another way of looking at the world and another way of looking at relationships. On our journey together we have witnessed and experienced unconditional love that has been beyond any experience that we had ever imagined.

We have done our best to have a relationship built on giving and on having as much interest in the other person as we have in ourselves. It is a relationship where we have to daily tear up our "scripts" for the other person. We are each attempting to listen to our own inner voice to tell us what to think, say, and do.

Our deep mutual desire to find another, better way of relating to each other, and to have greater harmony in all our relationships, has drawn us together to write this book.

There are those days when we still experience conflict and lack of harmony not only in our primary relationship but with other people in our lives. What is different now, however, is that we feel we are going in the right direction at last, and that we now have new tools that help us resolve problems and create the space for choosing peace instead of conflict, love instead of fear.